Dear Catherine Wheel

D & D PHILPOTT

Bonkers letters to

U.K Indie Bands

with genuine replies

Dear Catherine Wheel

D & D PHILPOTT

Bonkers letters to U.K Indie Bands with genuine replies

This Edition First Published By
Good Day Books October 2023
© D Dawson
Designed by D Dawson

ISBN: 9798386622954

Dear Catherine Wheel

D & D PHILPOTT

Bonkers letters to

U.K Indie Bands

with genuine replies

Special Thanks to:
Nick at Precious Recordings
Clare & Matt at Sarah Records
Tim Dorney
Iain Key
Amanda Austin
Freddie Valentine

Dear Catherine Wheel

D & D PHILPOTT

D & D Philpott are the aliases of two very ordinary people unconnected to the heady world of music and media, working with help from a worldwide social networking community to bring their nonsense to the attention of the artists.

Also still available from the same authors in paperback and on Kindle, via Amazon UK & Worldwide

  / The Philpotts

  @DerekPhilpott

  derek_and_dave_philpott

Dear Catherine Wheel

D & D PHILPOTT

DEDICATED TO

THE LONG-SUFFERING

LADY NEXT TO US ON

THE SOFA

Foreword

In a case of bluff calling bluff this book is a hilarious riposte and fiendish pin-pricking of the pomposity of pop culture. All the great music thrives on inflated ego and yet it's great to take the rise out its puffed up frithery. After the authors had sent out a series of mauling missives to random indie bands taking the piss out of their personal oeuvres with a series of pointed and frequently funny letters, they sat back and laughed and then forgot all about it. As a concept, it was hilarious, and the letters themselves would have been worthy on their own as a commentary on the self-conscious traps created by the magnetic yet strange world of band culture.

Stuffing the communications into their digital letterbox, the authors chuckled about their audacity and expected nothing in return, but were shocked when the bands started replying - often running with the joke with often witty ripostes, snarky rejoinders and pithy takedowns of their own lofty personae trashing halos and perceptions with their own sense of the ridiculous.

It makes for a great to and fro as it stalks right at the heart of perhaps the greatest British art form - irony. The machine gun missives and their sprightly comebacks that sit between acidic sarcasm and crayoned in fan madness somehow make the whole pop process seem far more human and the bottom line is that the art of snarkiness is very much alive in the ping pong of fan/band communication, and gives a unique snapshot into the very soul of independent music culture.

John Robb

"The legendary Philpotts entice the DIY recording, cardigan wearing, floppy fringed, guitar jangling, awkward shoe-gazing shufflers out of their bedrooms in this latest volume of letters. If you know your Nervous Twitch from your New FADS and Soup Dragons from your Shop Window this is an essential purchase"
Iain Key, Louder Than War

"Old Philpott is now too well known to catch anyone out, so his intrusive ramblings are treated with respect and often agonised over by people receiving their first letter in decades. Part of the charm of a book where you're rediscovering pretty much all of its inhabitants, is the civility and wit that erupts on virtually every page. Experience the pure joy of beginning with jovial bollocks, then multiplying that with cheerful cobblers."
'Mick Mirther'

"These books are a national institution and should have their own stage at Glastonbury."
Mark Stay, The Best Seller Experiment

"Recommended to any indie-pop fan who cherishes the impertinent nonsense of the Viz letters page"
Nige Tassell, author of Whatever Happened To The C86 Kids?

"Completely mad, of course! But this man goes to care homes and plays them Anarchy in the UK, so what's not to love?! A book with a heart as big as theirs. If you can't sneak this out of the shop without the assistant seeing, buy it: you won't regret it."
Bernie Keith, BBC

"It hits you with a heavy punch of nostalgia. As you read the letters from several generations' worth of indie bands you are let into their minds for a brief moment. Catching glimpses of what makes every band unique in their own special way. I would recommend this book to any music fan in the world for something you won't read in any other book"
Dave Watson, Britpop Buzz

"Quite a few of the people who contributed to this tome appear to be completely mad, but fortunately nowhere near as mad as Mr Philpott himself. Proud to have him as a member of our team at Radio Free Marseille and long may he prosper."

Richard Pearson, Station Controller

"A must read for even the most lackadaisical music fan, 'Dear Catherine Wheel' is truly a thing of beauty! Replies from all your Indie favourites, it'll have you rediscovering bands you thought you'd forgotten"

Paula Wiseman, The Divine Comedians

"What a crazy, wonderful love letter, or letters of love collection this is! What a thrill for all included!"

Jo Bartlett / Indie Through The Looking Glass

"The most amazing project I have ever come across - bonkers and beautiful in equal measures, it's a work of genius. From The Janitors to the Shop Assistants, The Philpotts have managed to track down and delve deep into the hidden messages within some of the greatest music written & recorded in the last 50 years. These bands were the soundtrack to 80s Britain, so it's wonderful to still remember them fondly and hear their thoughts on cryptic lyrics they thought no-one was paying attention to. Glad someone cares. The class of C86 had high standards."

David Eastaugh, The C86 Show

"Reading these exchanges, I was unexpectedly transported back to a packed Camden venue in about 1994, surrounded by people in bands, crew, fans and A&R, and everyone yelling conversations that made as much sense as these letters, over the sound of the latest Industry buzz trying to catch everyone's attention on stage... ahh, the smell of the Dublin Castle... the rammed bar and watered down beer of the Bull & Gate... it's uncanny! "

Marina, The Organ Magazine

"I'm glad I live in a world today that a publication exists where one can read overly petty missives to mostly obscure 20th century British indie music artists such as: The Monsoon Bassoon, Dolly Mixture, Hurrah! and David Devant & His Spirit Wife, but more satisfyingly enjoy the bands' good humoured replies.

The Philpotts' final glorious epistolary goes beyond levity, as I believe it is their affectionate tribute to all those unsung soldiers who many years ago bravely fought on the periphery of mainstream rock and pop.

Adorable.

Yeah, they're in the book too."
Paul Putner

CONTENTS

13

For a decade and a half the Philpotts have been getting under the skin of musical artistes. Picking up on glaring errors in their lyrics or sometimes getting completely the wrong end of the stick (perhaps to irritate things a little further) they totally misunderstand the meaning of the words 'poetic license'. Overfamiliar and always polite, yet demanding, this totally unqualified self-appointed "Compliance Department" often profer unwanted information regarding their day to day lives, and pepper their letters with references to the artists' other songs and lyrics, just to show off. Hundreds of missives have landed on the real and virtual doormats of musicians, worldwide. In return, these lyrical legends have exercised their right to reply however they like, often correcting and sometimes confirming the authors' summation of what went wrong... or right.

In this book they focus upon British indie artists from the past four decades. Here are the results.

A donation will be made to homeless charities from the profits of every copy of this book sold, as a thank you to the artists involved and to you, the reader.

"I think it's really, really poignant to say what an exceptional project this is. Reading - as I and lots of great songwriters that I know did - all of these absurd comments on our songs, really appeals to the absurdity in almost every musician. You want to kind of go, "Ah, I can do that! Bloody hell, listen to him!" So, you give it a go and it's really good fun. I sent their Deep Purple letter to my very good friend Roger Glover and he said "Oh, I'll not let him get away with it!"… So people were reacting in a way that they spend too much time touring and when you're touring you've got nothing to do for the other 23 hours; believe me I've done it. So you suddenly think this is a fantastic relief.. you know, I can mess with this."

Rupert Hine,
London Book Launch
The Dublin Castle 2018

Dear Flowered Up,

Yesterday's afternoon drink at a Camden 'gastropub' saw me nearly turn hysterically blue, choke on my pickled ~~egg rush~~ egg, and rush "Flapping" up to the bar to query whether I had been mistakenly billed for the adjacent table for 12.

I did try to haggle with the young barman ("I won't come down", he insisted) and so incredulously coughed up £18.50 for a Medium House Red and a BrewDog IPA before staggering out into the "Sunshine".

What with this, mounting fuel and shopping costs, and considering that the protagonist in your 1992 indie anthem "Weekender" was able at the time to sustain a three day binge on a blue collar wage, we strongly recommend that the work be re-recorded as "Swift Halfer", "Long Luncher" or, even as a healthy option, "Teetotaller", to reflect these austere times.

Yours, sincerely hope that you can "work it out".

D Philpott

Dear dear Derek,

Has it really been so long since we last corresponded? I suppose with that frightful Chinese flu business, it may well have been.

I'm afraid the gentrification of Camden has caused us all sorts of problems. For starters, where are us Dickensian street urchins supposed to park our barrows full of bootleg cassettes these days? £9/hour, I shit thee not.

The days of hiding up the gas manometers from the gabbers up the back of Kings Cross are long gone.. have you seen em? They've built flats INSIDE them at about 2 million a piece; Bagleys Warehouse, scene of many a crazy 'sweet I done about 40' nights? It's a bleedin' art gallery and artisan taco emporium. Jellied eels, pie and mash? Not on your nelly sunshine! Tapas and freshly knitted muesli.

We've all had to move to much more salubrious areas of the country now. No more duck and dive, bob and weave, shine your shoes guv'nor for us any more.. absolutely priced out of the area on all fronts. We've moved to Royal Leamington Spa, which whilst admittedly resembling the posher parts of Kensington seems to be inhabited by career alcoholics and spice smokers who want their country back; such a waste but reminds us of the rougher areas of Somerstown and the Regents Park Estate, which is nice.

Don't even start me on the price of fuel; what the hell are we gonna do when it all goes green? You can't siphon electricity out of a battery can ya? Since Brexit we can't even maintain a good lunchtime binge let alone a weekend on the jack 'n jills and the showbiz sherbet.

Weekender, weekender! Go out! Have a lunchtime! Doesn't have the same ring.

I blame the lettuce.

Tim Dorney

Dear The ~~Odd Job Men~~ Janitors,

What Can I Say, The ~~Caretakers~~ Janitors? The Fallen One seemed to avoid the "Rest Of The World" in the 80s, but there _is_ a report - "Only One" - from a Charlie Daniels that he went down to Georgia in 1979.

Mr. Mark E Smith reported "Lucifer Over Lancashire" in 1985, whilst in 1986 you, The ~~Custodians~~ Janitors, insisted that "The Devil's Gone To Whitley Bay".

As "Time Goes On", I am "Nowhere" near fathoming where he's "Going To Be" next! Indeed, he may be

"Halfway To A Happening" right now, embarking on another brilliant year of mini breaks and "Family Fantastic" package deals.. and marvelling that it's "Good To Be The King" of The Underworld.

Yours, hoping I've typed "The Right Stuff",

D Philpott

Dear Mr Philpott,

Many thanks for your correspondence. It is indeed a little known fact that Beelzebub was indeed a fan of the staycation long before it became a necessity of austerity. In truth this was not the first manifestation of the Dark Lord on the east coast - remember his servant Dracula's famous weekend break to Whitby and the proliferation of bathing witches in Berwick-upon-Tweed as reported by no lesser figure than King James VI.

We must be vigilant and look for signs of his return. Where might he try next; sleepy Hunstanton, bustling Yarmouth or seedy Skegness? He truly is the master of disguise and also a big fan of leaden skies and chilly beaches.

Yours ever vigilant,

Janitors

Dear The ~~Horizontal Homies~~ Flatmates,

"Heaven Knows" you pop stars do like a metaphor, The ~~Condo Comrades~~ Flatmates, but "did I misunderstand"? There's a risk "You're Gonna Cry" if you can't tell me why all that's left of me is in your empty head.

I am fully intact The ~~Duplex Droogs~~ Flatmates, so that's "oh, when it falls apart". Furthermore (and "This Is Reality"), even were any body part to be in your heart - which you can't get me out of, apparently - or cranium, the latter could by no means be considered empty.

Although it "seemed that everything was planned" The ~~Apartment Amigos~~ Flatmates, this is, "Trust Me", as bad as when Mr. Young told me I take a piece of him with me every time I go away!

Yours, "Thinking Of You", with "nothing left to say",

D. Philpott

Dear Mr. Phliptopp,

We think you might be labouring under a misapprehension with regard to Mr. Young. Indeed, in response to Paul Young's slightly disturbing and veggie-phobic "Every time you go away, you take a piece of meat with you", we were prompted to write what proved to be The Flatmates' biggest hit, "Slimmer". Playing upon listener's insecurities and conforming to the public's desire for romantic pop, we wrote the lyrics, "See me slimmer in the night, like a firefly burning bright, slimmer baby, slimmer...for your love".

The success of "Slimmer" was no surprise to those who had followed The Flatmates' progress through songs like "Tell Me Why" ("Tell me why it is you cry, why it is your tummy lies..."), and a theme (some would say obsession) that continues into 2020's The Flatmates album (released through the Subway Organization, SUBORG 18CD. Purchase or download from localunderground.co.uk), on titles such as "Cheese...So Bad For You" and "Something In My Pie".

Rest assured, Mr. Phlopalott, that we can certainly sympathise with your plight, no doubt caused by decades of standing too close to the speaker stacks at Indie Pop Concerts. Indeed, I recently overheard an exchange between two members of The Flatmates upon disembarking from the tour bus that went something like "Blimey, isn't it windy?", "No, I'm sure it's Thursday", "Me too. When does the bar open?"

We therefore have pleasure in supplying for your assessment a sample of our newest item of merchandise, the EarMate 3000. Discrete hearing assistance for discerning indie-folk, branded with "THE FLATMATES" in 56pt Impact typeface, and a picture of a jumping girl straight off the cover of "Happy All The Time" (which I'm sure you will be). If not completely satisfied with the EarMate 3000 please return using the enclosed address sticker (otherwise the invoice is enclosed in the separate brown envelope, cash or bank transfer. No, we don't take Green Shield stamps or Luncheon Vouchers.)

May I thank you for your continuing patronage, which has paid for our dinners since 1986.

Yours,

The Fatmates

Dear Fuzzbox,

Firstly, as regards your complaint, "I can't even get to Hell", I would recommend heading out on to any junction on the M25 at 3pm-ish on a Friday and driving around the whole ruddy thing to arrive back where you started. We have AA Cover for both the UK and abroad in the event of a "Big Bang!" or Breakdown, so it's nice to see that you've been sensible enough to be "Calling International Rescue"... and you should be easy to trace given that the Orbital Motorway is not "off the beaten track".

On an unrelated matter concerning another benevolent organisation best known by its initials, I'm afraid that to employ a domestic rodent as an offensive weapon, even in self defence, is worthy of an official report to the R.S.P.C.A.. Especially considering that you've got a fuzzbox that you're prepared to use, I'm dismayed that Freddie tried to strangle you but you hit him back with your pet rat.

Yours, anticipating "Fuzzy Ramblings",

D Philpott

Dear Mr Philpott,

I don't drive I'm afraid but even so I am very concerned that you have taken out breakdown cover with a bunch of alcoholics. Whilst I'm not one to impose "Rules and Regulations" on others I do think it prudent to take care of one's "Self" whilst driving in our green and pleasant land. The weather can be so unpredictable; it's not always "Pink Sunshine" and often people can find themselves "Walking on Thin Ice". I take a sensible approach and always have "International Rescue" on speed dial in case I get stuck. I know it's easy for me to say but when you're in a pickle:

Philpott pick the proper people!

As for the matter concerning the rat, that was not me but Vix. Her and Freddie have history and are prone to violent outbursts. I've had to report them myself on numerous occasions. Actually, it's a disgrace and quite frankly an embarrassment. On a technical note, the type of Fuzzbox Vix and I have is pretty useless in a combat situation. The only projectile I have managed to launch from it is a ping pong ball and even then it's quite tricky to do that during a brawl.

I hope I've brought some clarity to your investigations.

Maggie, off of Fuzzbox

Dear ~~The Astronaut Trio~~ Spacemen 3,

I fear, "Any Way That You Want Me" to phrase it, that you are literally "Playing With Fire" pertaining to your proposed solar digit singeing expedition.

You might have "been to some far out places", but to expect to "burn your fingers on the sun" rather than suffer massive doses of "Transparent Radiation" and be fried to a crisp, is like jumping off a diving board hoping just to get your toenails a bit moist.

There is no chance, ~~Rocket Pilot Trinity~~ Spacemen 3, that you will "Come Down Easy" and "Call The Doctor" for "The Perfect Prescription" and be "Feelin' Just Fine". I want you right now to turn your "Starship" around and abort this "Suicide" Mission, lest you be "Walking With Jesus" far sooner than anticipated!

Yours, promising that "Things'll Never Be The Same",

D Philpott

Dear Mr Philpott,

Thank you for your recent letter. I always welcome well meaning advice, especially when it arrives 30 years too late. You may rest assured that any journeys into "space" were largely imaginary, therefore rendering any of the usual "safety" measures associated with traditional space travel completely useless. There is little point in an expensive shielding system to protect the inhabitants of the vessel from cosmic radiation when the vessel in question is actually a sofa in a small terraced house and the inhabitants are unlikely to leave the comforts of the "starship" unless they run out of cigarette papers or anti gravity pills.

Luckily for us, inner space was a much closer prospect than boring old outer space and it was generally much cheaper to get there. Do you know where inner space is Mr Philpott? Just in from the nose and slightly north of the eyebrows, turn left at the newsagents, ignore that grinning cat and gird yer loins. You will be there in no time. Or will you? Perhaps it doesn't matter.

Space is big, time is oblong and it is only for those of us stupid enough to try to and navigate the unmentionables of that eternity with no map, dented derring-do and a vague sense of impending doom. If you ever feel compelled to exploration, I suggest you put on some soothing Sunday evening TV, pop a co-codamol and do a shot of night nurse. You will soon be "losing touch with your mind" and you should be at the "other side" in no time. Don't forget to take a packed lunch.

I wish you the best of luck in your endeavours.

Sincerely,

Will Carruthers ....

(very much ex) Spacemen3, Spiritualized, Deaf Skeletons, Brinjar Jonestown Moussaka, Guaranteed ugly and occasional ditch digger.

Dear Pele,

Re: The Sport of Kings

Given the tight security surrounding the Royal Family (not Ricky Tomlinson's) we are surprised that you exposed Her Majesty's displeasure at her Windsor Greys and Cleveland Bays, prior to her demise.

Her subjects' understanding that the Queen is unhappy today with her horses is reasonable, but your revelations relating to her eviscerating a ruminant could, if you let the truth in, cause "Fireworks" within the "Empire".

We therefore implore you, if you wish to continue living here in the land of the free, not to disclose that the Queen is with her children today tearing up the heart of a stag.

Yours, Bucking(ham) The Trend,

D Philpott

Dear Mr. Philpott,

Now I know since privatisation our formerly glorious postal service has gone to the dogs but still your letter's arrival came as an immense shock. Sent, as it must have been, before our wonderful monarch put down her knife and fork, your words have inadvertently acted as a terrible jolting reminder that she is no longer with us.

Before replying to you I sent a stern and somewhat angry note to the postal service pointing out that the tardiness of your letter's delivery felt like I was reliving her painful demise all over again. Yet, unlike last time when my sorrow was soothed by the communal outpouring of national love (many of my fellow singers were clearly as distressed as I was), this time it felt awfully solitary.

So much so that all of my former youthful (and frankly uncouth) Republican utterances are regrettably of a mortal embarrassment to me now. To underline my allegiance to the new King and somehow try to repair my childlike proclamations of yesteryear I should like to wish Charles and his beautiful Queen every luck in future evicerations of whichever animal they wish to fillet and skillet.

All living things on this sceptred isle belong to the throne, and we would all do well to remember that.

Ian Prowse

Liverpool, August 2023.

Dear ~~Gasoline Gut Feeling~~ That Petrol Emotion,

If you've seen the film about that 70's bloke on a highwire, not in Circusville but "Under The Sky (Live)", ~~Four Star Sentiment~~ That Petrol Emotion, you'll perhaps sense his "Natural Kind Of Joy".

Being a "Hot Head" who "can't stop falling" foul of the law, it's a good thing that he took "Every Little Bit" of the stunt very slowly, by creeping to the crossing between the Twin Towers "Tightlipped", and teetering between "Tension" and a "Fun Time".

Aware that he must fight this comedown or plummet 1,350 feet to literally become a "Tired Shattered Man", the bottom line is that Philippe Petit had no lattice protection, That ~~Diesel Desire~~ Petrol Emotion. Your declaration therefore that "you can't walk a tight rope without a safety net" is, sadly, "A Million Miles Away" from the truth.

Should you feel the "Compulsion" to address this, I look forward to hearing from you "Sooner Or Later".

Yours, awaiting your "big decision",

D Philpott

Dear Phil Pott,

No error! Shut that crazy mouth!

For what it's worth, Petit actually wore a tiny parachute so your declaration is factually incorrect, you big deadbeat. You seem to have a blind spot about this. The bottom line is that Petit was an infinite thrillseeker and a deep, sensitized soul but he didn't want to die. Sooner or later he knew his secret would come out but he remained tight-lipped about the secret 'chute.

Your letter doesn't make much sense now in light of the

above info; in fact it's a big mess of words. Maybe you had a headstagger when you wrote it! Maybe your belly bugs were playing up that day! And by the way, what were those gnaw marks on the side of your letter? Was your dog hungry? Definitely not a genius move! Sorry to detonate your dreams but don't contact us again!

Yours

Raymond, Gorman

That Petrol Emotion

Dear Catherine Wheel,

"I Confess" to discovering your "Black Metallic" song when searching for a Touch Up Kit. It was a "Painful Thing" to do after I pranged my Nissan Juke today, incurring a "Broken Head"light, shallow scuffs in the outer "Texture" and some deep scratches all the "Waydown" to the bodywork.

I don't mind the personification of your own car per se. Telling it "your skin is black metallic" does not imply you to be a "Crank", and "Ballad Of A Running Man" - obviously being parked up with the engine idle - is not necessarily indicative of an "Empty Head". I must take issue though with the automobile "saying" that "it's easy when it's faster". Despite what we want to believe in, speed limits exist for a reason Catherine, especially in residential areas.

I do agree however that the vehicle "can't stay all day under the covers". To protect the paintwork and "Chrome" when stationary is very sensible, but to drive about with the windscreen and back window fully obscured is, quite frankly, "Shocking".

Finally, should you suffer similar collision damage, and unless there exists within you the capacity to change your opinion that "Indigo Is Blue" , I heartily recommend the Halfords Colour Code Chart.

"Goodbye".

Derek Philpott

Dear Mr Philpott,

Thank you for your very informative missive. I am very sorry that you have had to visit Halfords for a touch-up kit; quite "Shocking" to be honest, or am I being "Shallow"? However, it really is a "Lifeline" to have such a magnificent car repair emporium at hands' reach. It really is "What we all want to believe in".

I do, however, have an alternative answer to your "Car" repair "Pain". I know an enterprising young woman; "She's my friend", you know. She has just run a stall at "My Exhibition" of car repair products and procedures.

She was at first reluctant to take part, but I said "Show Me Mary" and she did. The "sparks really did fly" and she did "Receive" much praise, rubbing "Salt" into the competition's wounds. She would be very willing to come up for a "mouthful of air" and take a look at the damage to your vehicle.

Between you, me, and "these four walls", she is very talented, hard working and hates the "Idle Life", so should be able to "Heal" your poor damaged vehicle. I hope this letter isn't too "Saccharine", but she really is "Harder than I am" when it comes to vehicle repair.
Good day.

Catherine

Hello, Goodbye Mr. Mackenzie,

I am trying to keep my time on the computer "Down To The Minimum", but did chance upon your song "The Rattler" whilst googling American venomous snakes… by which I do not mean some of the more recent historical Presidential Candidates.

Initially interpreting "a rattling boy" to be some kind of "Mystery Train" full of crockery, it now appears that the clanky noxious male, or "Ugly Child", could be Spotify founder Daniel Ek.

That he is rattling "through the countryside" and "coming down the line" - clear references to capacious coverage of fibre-optic broadband - is patently obvious. His accountability not for "Good Deeds" but instead giving "HMV", and most musicians, many a "Bad Day" via "eating them, cheating them" of realistic royalty payments is also well-documented.

Your allusion to the alleged megalomaniac "Sick Boy" having no social media presence - "I don't like people to know my face" - is bang on, whilst "stationary as a stream" and "but I can't take you all the way" both admirably address the issues of constant buffering.

I sincerely hope that my discovery of these "Secrets" is not "Troubling You", and that you will not be "Tongue Tied" in your response to this letter, if indeed you decide not to "Trash It".

Yours, staying on track,

D. Philpott

Dear Mr. Philpott,

We know not of what you talk. You are way out of the ballpark and grasping the wrong end of the candlestick. There is no mystery, and there is no train full of crockery – that's just a crock of s***! Round the bend.

We find ourselves in very troubling times, in dark places. The former Prince of Wales – (Yes! THAT Prince Of Wales) – has just been crowned King of little England and, like the Titanic, we are lost at sea.

"We can have but one feeling on the matter – contempt for thrones and for all who bolster them up."

This rattling boy you insist on dredging up from the past knows nothing of fibre optics, logarithms and the metaverse. He is a much simpler construct, a relic from more innocent times. It is not a mouse, small and cold, he holds in his right hand but something much more vital. He remains forever, blissfully, suspended in his own realm, aimless in extreme. He has no ken of your kind of stream.

What we wouldn't give to join him, to have our heads in the sand rather than attempt to make any sense at all of the here and now, never mind the there and then. But the clock is ticking, Tik-Tok Tik-Tok, and there's much to do . . . How many wise men does it take to make AI, do you know? Do you know?

Fin Wilson

7th May 2023 (the day of some Coronation or other apparently)

Dear The ~~Winnie Twigs~~ Pooh Sticks,

I write concerning your second degree of separation staple "I Know Someone Who Knows Someone Who Knows Alan McGee Quite Well".

In my experience, being matey with someone in showbiz who can definitely help with your career will all be fine until you ask them for something which can definitely help with your career.

A schoolfriend of mine, Jacinta Trevidi, used to have coffee with Ben Kingsley, well-noted for portraying "Heroes And Villains". He told her in 1979 that he was "Working On A Beautiful Thing" about a peace-loving man who united India. When she asked if she could be an extra in the New Delhi crowd scene or even just attend "Opening Night" he asked her for "Just Another Minute" to go to the gents and she didn't see him again until Sexy Beast.

That said, I doubt that she can be trusted. When I visited her to collect my amp, she showed me her Telecaster, boasting it to be the one Jimmy Page used on the million seller "Dazed and Confused". Its Trade Mark Of Quality was for a 1982 Squier (it's a copy), so I may have been taken for an "Optimistic Fool".

Yours, hoping that you are not ~~tiggered~~ triggered,

D. Philpott

D! You OK?

I saw you outside. Ha! You know Jacinta! I was in school with her sister, Rubella. Get her to tell you "about the time when...". Just ask her that. Tell her I said to ask; she'll know what I'm talking about!

I was thinking about those two just today, oddly. Rubella actually did know Alan McGee: she used to go into the office most days on the way home from the old St. Mary Magdelene Girls Academy when it was just up the road. She was trying to persuade McGee to send her and Jacinta out as Baby Amphetamine because the real girls didn't want to do it and, well, no-one would've been any the wiser. Anyway, ask Jacinta about "the time when…". If you can get her to tell you, you'll think it's the best story you've ever heard. She won't, but ask her anyway.

And another 'ha!': I knew Ben Kingsley briefly. Small world! I'd auditioned to be in that 'Bugsy' thing he did and I got the part! Bad timing, though, as just then the band was getting really busy, so in the end I couldn't do it. We stayed in touch for a little while after that, but you know how it goes. Because of knowing me, he bought a Pooh Sticks record and absolutely hated it. Anyway, he was nice, I liked him.

Got no story about Jimmy Page.

But anyway, yes, I agree about career-help. Knowing the right people at the right time really counts. My favourite bit of advice we ever had was from our new manager in 1992: he said "Don't do what Slash does" (his other client was Guns 'n Roses) although, even then, if we'd been told this before our Japan tour Hue might not have got himself arrested in Kyoto. More bad timing! Still, it was useful for the last couple of years of the band, and it's a motto that's been keeping me personally out of (too much) trouble ever since.

So look, gotta go, but thanks for the nice actual letter this time. It makes a change from reading the obscenities fingered into the dirt on the Suburu every morning, and your spelling is improving!

Love
Trudi xxx

Dear The Beloved,

You've got me thinking each and every time I've mulled over the conundrum within your selective celebrity school register simulation song, "Hello". It really is "A Beautiful Waste Of Time".

After "Forever Dancing" around the issue and sitting "On The Fence", sincerely hoping to wake up soon to the solution, I finally deferred to our Art Teacher acquaintance, Franny Braithwaite; the only girl I knew capable of examining it to "The Last Detail".

She asks that you "Please Understand" blue to be a primary colour, ie. one which can't be made by mixing pigments. Green, combining two primary colours, can be achieved from a base colour of lapis by adding iron oxide to varying degrees in "Sweet Harmony", depending on what end result is "Good For You".

When asked therefore if she can spot the difference lying between the colours blue and green, she could "come on down" to "Just One Thing", and it was called yellow; not, as you erroneously claim, "blue is blue and it always will be".

Please "Surprise Me", The Beloved, and deliver me, plain to see, a reply of more than "A Hundred Words".

Yours, Unanswered Still,

D Philpott

Dear Mr Philpott,

How very kind of you to write a letter answering the question posed in the verses of the song 'Hello'.

I do hope it hasn't eluded you for 30+ years?

Virtually all the attention focussed on the song was regarding the names in the choruses. Celebrity School register is a witty description. Also potentially a concept for a reality TV show in some guise.. not based on my list I hasten to add, not least because 9 have subsequently died. It almost became 10 but thankfully Mr Rushdie survived.

The actual meaning of the lyric, and therefore the conundrum, was about the political appropriation of environmentally-friendly policies for electoral gain. A deep mistrust of the sudden championing of Green ideas by Blue ideologues.

I am glad to say now how wrong I was.

I am overjoyed to see that Climate Change and the impending disaster for the planet have been firmly tackled and become the number one priority for society.

But I digress.

Yes, you are correct. Or rather your friend Franny is correct and has thankfully freed you from eternal puzzlement. If addressed as about colour itself then the riddle is solved.

However, if you had been a reader of Smash Hits magazine in 1990 when the song was originally released, you would have discovered the same answer. They ran a competition to win a raft of Beloved goodies and the opportunity to spend an afternoon with us in the recording studio.

As you can imagine, there were a lot of entries but the tie-breaker used to select the ultimate winner was the riddle in the song. The most unique response would claim the prize.

The winner was a lovely young boy from Exeter called Christopher who sent a cassette tape of him singing the answer. Interestingly he used the same phraseology as yourself.

He sang "It was called Yellow". The tune was rather good.

When he came to the studio he was very keen on the process and had an aptitude for music. We gave him encouragement and wished him well. I have occasionally wondered what became of him?

Again, thank you for taking the time to write to me. I do hope you are not similarly absorbed by lyrics in other peoples' songs because that could be quite overwhelming!

Best wishes to you Sir!

Jon Marsh

Dear Cud,

Although not "Not Necessarily Evil", you lead me, "no bones about it", to wholeheartedly concur that you should be trusted least with the finest beast.

Sometimes rightly, sometimes wrongly, prospective tenants are fed up and NOT made up as they struggle to settle into their rented accommodations thanks to a ban on pets by some "Little Comedian".

The mystery deepens therefore pertaining to your rich and strange endangered species' dungeon. One wonders how you have managed to keep tigers "Down Down" in the cellar since June last year without your landlord going "Through The Roof".

The incarcerated felines "really should return back to the jungle" and, once again, your assertion that I won't hide the crimes that you've done is correct – as well as a head full of loose change you may before tomorrow also have a house full of 'coppers'.

I typed most of this while horizontal in bed, but although I was lying, I told the truth!

Yours, yet to "Slip Away",

D. Philpott

Dear D,

You seem to have more familiarity with the CUD band's lyrics than our singer. Before you call in the dogs, or the RSPCA, I wish to explain our singer's predilection for referencing our animal brethren in his song words.

When CUD first started, and indeed every day since, we have assumed our accidental success was sure not to last. This was the only thing we were correct about. So, we all made plans for the future. For me, it was investing my humble share of song-writing royalties in a dental hygiene and manicure franchise - "Tooth and Nail". Mike and Gogs have pooled their profits into developing a cure for shindigs. Carl, the song singer, had a dream not unlike that of Gerald Durrell, to set up his own menagerie, and it is to this he refers to obliquely in his lyrics.

While the CUD Zoo had a humble origin - a bowl of Sea Monkeys and a lucky rabbit's foot - since we began including "random rare, ideally endangered species" on our tour rider, Carl's collection has increased exponentionally and has taken over the East Wing of his West Yorkshire country pile.

The tiger you refer to - Geoff - was only with us for a short while before his stripes washed off and he was revealed as a pine marten. But Geoff promises to be a star-attraction, along with the Kimono Dragon, the Fender Jaguars and the leggy mambo, when the appropriate licences are supplied, the TB erased, and the Puttnam Petting Zoo finally opens in Spring 2024.

In quarantine,

Will CUD

Dear Salad,

On the "Inside Of My Head", Salad, I am "Nowhere Near" comprehending the "Wayward Thinking" of today and am "In The Dark". I find such matters "Problématique" and I "Wanna Be Free" of my misconceptions, which do not "Make Me Laugh".

I therefore respect that "It's For You" - "You Got The Job" - to decide how to exist rather than "Being Human".

In your case, you choose not to be a "Poor Peach", but state, "I'm now an apple.. so edible", certainly not plucked from an 'Evergreen' tree, but worthy of inclusion in a Waldorf Salad.

That "Suits Me Fine", ~~Vegan Medley~~ Salad, and I urge you to embrace your deciduous persona and declare "I Identify As A Golden Delicious", or, if I am somehow mistaken, "I identify as an Apple Macintosh", which rather negates your claim that "we should all carry pens".

"What Do You Say About That"?

"I Want You" to please "Come Back Tomorrow" with your reply.

Yours, awaiting "Details",

D Philpott

Well Mr Philpott, you have certainly swotted up on all things Salad. Do you wish for us to embrace you and whisper sweet onions into your ear? Do you want us to name our next pet lettuce after you? Or do you indeed wish for us to start a Salad word play battle, because we can assure you sir, that we will beetroot you into tiny quinoa pieces, until you will be nothing more than a man in a box... (you kent).

Let us keep you in the dark no longer, and commence by suggesting that your ma is so fat, she is not only a size more woman than her next door neighbour, but her clothes look so diminished on her that she could be mistaken for a beefy tomato in a tiny pea coat.

Furthermore, we bet that when you and Mrs Philpott take time to escape, tossing aside all your relationship dust (and the fact that nothing much happens anymore when your aubergine meets her roasted vegetables), you leave your shepherd's isle to go sailing to a tropical island because you DON'T KNOW HOW TO FLY!

We do also need to urgently address why we are indeed an apple in a line. It is because we love the doctor, and of all the princes and all the fools we choose him, but alas we know the blue cold eyed muscleman will never be ours.

We hope we'll never meet as we imagine you might want to shove us under the wrapping paper and turn us into pulp (oh sorry, wrong band), unless you will allow us to clear our name another terrible day.

Lastly a few words of advice - firstly DON'T expect things not to be scary...and secondly DO drink the elixir.

Yours grated cheesefully,

Salad

Dear The Cravats,

As a regular viewer of "Nightmare Tenants, Slum Landlords", I almost cried onto my Lenovo Thinkpad (or shed "Tears On My Machine") upon learning that there's a great big hole underneath your home.

If indeed "the ruskies have invaded by going underground" to "Bury The Wild" nefarious plans, then your domestic abyss might be one ~~Pressure Seller~~ Prussia Cellar in a thousand ~~Pre-Sinks~~ Precincts. Sadly, The ~~Necker Chiefs~~ Cravats, "You're Driving Me" to the conclusion that these blurred "Power Lines" could be The Very Things leading to "Whooping Sirens" and our "Ceasing To Be".

We must be "All On Standby".

It seems that there Is *No* International Rescue, The ~~Throat Garments~~ Cravats. When Will We Fall?

Yours, 100 Percent committed to a ~~Batter~~ Better House,

D Philpott

To Mr. Philpott:

Sir, your concern for our historical plight does you credit and your thoughts about the obvious wider implications chime with our thoughts entirely. You clearly have DEEP INSIGHT and are A PRINCE AMONG MEN.

To bring you up to date: THE GREAT BIG HOLE (as we have dubbed it) has grown over time and we believe it is now what the boffins call a SUPERMASSIVE BLACK HOLE, from which nothing can escape, not even light (let alone our humble selves, Messrs. Dallaway and Shend).

We operate a CONSTANT vigil, taking turns to survey the phenomenon, but still NOTHING is visible in the blackness. We understand that the 'event horizon' is populated by ever increasing volumes of motor vehicles circumnavigating the traffic island on which our abode stands. You are probably ahead of us, Sir, in thinking that surely such traffic will inevitably be sucked through our home into the void. IMAGINE OUR CONSTERNATION!

Whilst recognising that there will be NO assistance from either the local authorities, or the national government (unbelievably, The Welsh Assembly HAS NOT EVEN ACKNOWLEDGED OUR COMMUNICATIONS), we remain hopeful. Events have caused us to think again about International Rescue. Mr. Jeff Tracy HAS CONTACTED US via the YouTube, and although he and his talented offspring are clearly very busy thwarting plots by foreigners like Mr. Hood, WE BELIEVE that when he gets a spare minute he will send Virgil and T2 to help (perhaps with a giant concrete mixer in the pod; I have never seen such a vehicle on the conveyor, but they must have at least one tucked away following the MASSIVE construction job which is now Tracy Island). FURTHERMORE our predicament is a perfect fit for the type of foreigner plot-foiling this esteemed family specialises in.

Thank you once again for your support and kind words. THANK GOD there is someone out there who understands.

With all good wishes,

R.R. Dallaway

Second Reply

Dear Danny Philpitt,

Firstly, how the hell did you get my address?

The whole point of living 'off grid' is that Gary Grid has no idea where you are. That includes Percy Postman, Ian Inland Revenue and Tommy TV Licence.

Maybe you used one of those data scam fish bots that are all too prevalent these days but they aren't ~~infallauable~~ infallible and I can assure you my Natwest Bank Account number is NOT really:

65892273
(sort code 23-58-12).

Anyway, what's done is done so let's move on.

My esteemed cohort R.R. Dallaway has gone into great depth to explain the circumstances surrounding THE GREAT BIG HOLE and as he is a respected expert in the field of geological anomalies there is nothing I can add.

In fact, it is difficult to know how to respond to your meandering and somewhat incoherent letter but as someone who also watched "Nightmare Tenants, Slum Landlords" as well as far superior TV fare such as "Say Yes To The Dress" before fleeing the modern world and constructing the bracken covered yurt in which I now dwell with only the nighttime squawk of voles as my companion ...

… er, I can't remember where this was going but I'm afraid that often happens living alone in the wilderness with no human contact (apart, of course, from the giant purple semi-transparent Jimmy Tarbuck that joins me for soil burgers beside the campfire every Tuesday eve).

Suffice to say, we can all enjoy a visit to Hoorahland Bemusement Park but please remember the rides aren't free and why does Ralph Fiennes pronounce his first name 'Ralph' instead of 'Ralph' like most people?

Kind regards

The Shend

Dear ~~Sonogram~~ Ultrasound,

I chanced upon your anti-ageing 'infomercial', "Stay Young", this morning whilst investigating wrinkle cream for Mrs. Philpott, and must suggest, in order that your target demographic "Can't Say No", that you ~~maybelline~~ maybe lean towards "Getting Better".

Even pensioners today demand instant results, my baby preview-monikered friends, hence to infer a passage of time dreaded by many elderly people, and stipulate that "all this will be theirs in the future", is hardly cause to "celebrate the new"!

Sadly, the 'Dragon's Den'-repelling tagline, "You'll be dead and gone before you know how it works" only serves to exacerbate the likelihood of any potential sales investment disappearing down a "Black Hole".

You have our "Best Wishes" Ultrasound but we must go now as for some reason we have an overwhelming urge to watch an old episode of "One Born Every Minute".

Yours, hoping that you have not gone to seed,

D Philpott

Dear Mr. (and Mrs.) Philpott,

We are sorry to hear that your results have been less than satisfactory. However, I would like to reaffirm that the treatment should be applied only to the face and neck and not anywhere near the aforementioned "Black Hole" and its subsequent sensitive areas. May I suggest that this might be where you have "come undone" and thus terribly likely to "scream all you like".

My advice to all your boys (and all your girls) is to rinse it under a tap, or bidet if you are continentally inclined, and "in the future" follow the provided instructions more carefully.

We do hope that there was no longer lasting damage to the above (and indeed below) areas, and if problems persist may I recommend our latest product, "Sovereign", which will "wash clean your filthy rotten souls", and "bring life to the fecund few", or, perhaps, our newer "God's Gift" range, which brings relief to a range of ailments including 'lockjaw', 'queasy sickness', and even a 'swollen rage', which we all suffer from as we get older.

Your humble servants,

Ultrasound

Dear The ~~Cyclone Saxophone~~ Monsoon Bassoon,
My nephew Dorian started work laying patios in Wiltshire last week, The ~~Cloudburst Clarinet~~ Monsoon Bassoon, and his first client was a very pleasant chap. Sadly, "In The Nice Man's Back Garden", he rolled all over the Flamingo Lawn and crashed the "Digger" into an ornamental pyramid, damaging the "Blue Junction" box and smashing the windscreen.

Luckily, The ~~Hurricane Harmonica~~ Monsoon Bassoon, "Mr Chip In Chippenham" was able to come out straight away and put a new one in, but Dorian was sacked on the spot, went absolutely bonkers, and was immediately succeeded by a new apprentice.

He therefore agrees The ~~Tin Whistle Tempest~~ Monsoon Bassoon, that "like glass you may crack", but given that both he and the JCB window were easily supplanted, your comment, "unlike glass you'll not be replaced" is not right, "Wise Guy".

Yours, hoping you'll give me something or anything,

D Philpott

Dear Mr Philpott,

A sorry but all too familiar tale if ever I heard one.

Like your nephew, I too was once a young man.

Feckless and idle, during the era in which we collectively fabricated our now largely forgotten 'Great Work', myself and several other 'Cyclonians' were regularly tasked with 'manual labour'. The digging of trenches, a 'low responsibility' calling, was a necessity to supplement the meagre income we barely attained from our ill-constructed doggerel and musical illiteracy, upon which far more responsible adult men would presumably 'construct patios'.

A fool's errand at best, each day's labour was executed through a Laudanum haze, the crippling boredom and ennui of our lot barely enhanced by an assortment of tinctures and tonics which would exchange hands with some frequency. When finally arriving at the blessed 'going home time', the emaciated 'cash in hand' remittance would swiftly find its way into the pocket of our local publican, a disreputable lollygagger known to us only as 'Tache Twitcher'.

While I cannot speak for my fellow 'Harmonicons', and God knows I have tried, much less Dorian, what scant wisdom I could glean from my disconsolate time in 'the trade' was that, as with the ignominious sphere of 'Lysergic Rock', *they're all at it.*

I therefore respectfully suggest you ask about the contents of your nephew's pockets before pointing fingers, sir.

Yours regrettably,

Kavus Torabi

Dear Corduroy,

Finlay Bedford, one of the "Boys Wonder" of Holiday Trip underwriters, can usually skirt alert, but I fear his "Data" may put "The Frighteners" on you.

He agrees that "it's getting much harder to keep our faith", but failing to disclose that you "walked with a zombie and took a fantastic journey" may cause any submitted claim to "fall apart before too long".

It's all very well that, "no one tells you of the trouble with insurance cover, check the small print everytime you take another lover", but "High Havoc" could ensue should your undead travelling companion "Chow Down" on your good selves leaving no "Man Alive", Finlay adds.

He insists that no "Paper Money" or "Blackmail" inducement will run like clockwork, man.

Yours, hoping that you "Don't Wait For Monday",

D Philpott

Dear 'D.'

As the Buddha famously said - 'all life is sorry, it's name is desire.'

Possessions are a burden, the accumulation of which may require an expensive insurance policy to ease the stress and worry of losing your precious items.

I choose, for this reason, to live a Spartan existence, navigating life with little more than a clean pair of socks and a travel toothbrush. I remain uninsured.

Your letter cites lyrics from the Corduroy composition 'Supercrime', which is not, as you have mistakenly assumed, a pointless rant against high street retail insurance cover; that would be ridiculous. The song was in fact a crass attempt to garner synchronisation income from inclusion on 'That's Life', a television show presented by Esther Rantzen and Cyril Fletcher. Unfortunately this was futile as the BBC decommissioned the program in 1994, four years before the song was written.

Regards

R

Dear ~~Captain Constantine~~ Earl Brutus,

Even in a "Second Class War", I sincerely doubt that the British Army's elite counter-terrorism unit would embark on a "Universal Plan" encumbered with platform boots, feather boas and hippie flares.

Furthermore, ~~Czar Caesar~~ Earl Brutus, to give away their position by blaring out Slade and The Sweet, and, for that matter, declaring: "Your Majesty We Are Here", would surely render the phrases "Don't Die Jim" and "Life's Too Long" redundant.

Therefore, ~~Duke Domitian~~ Earl Brutus, I look forward to "your own reaction" to "The SAS And The Glam That Goes With It".

Yours, hoping you "Don't Leave Me Behind Mate",

D Philpott

Dr Mr Philpott,

The inept sucking 73% dead without excuse mickle shat narrow cast underclassed slackheaded charvers poodles on £500 a day value subtracted over-raked attitudinal tarred slum palace estates brutal thickness (side stepped) earl brutus refuse to bomb London yero zero national inter-dim wholly wooly theme parked mobile senescence tarzan illusion stunted battery-hen savoirs emulated novelty generation repetition docile sick metaphorabject north saracen ultra feeble minded martyr/mocha jet set eat fish and chips eat shit music and chips

Now wash your hands

Kind regards,

Karl Brutus

(We knew you'd say that! D & D Philpott)

Dear Amelia Fletcher off of Talulah Gosh,

I mistakenly found your "indie combo" whilst I was googling Tallulah Gorge, which is also part of a split rock formation.

I tried to convey to Mr. Sting that a hundred billion bottles seems rather a round figure. Also, a cursory perusal on "Yahoo Answers" revealed that, counting at one number per second, non-stop, it would take him about 31 years, 8 months, to reach a billion, which, multiplied by one hundred, amounts to 376.66 years.

Similarly, your claim of mass hysteria in the smiling face of a young lady by a blackboard holding a knitted clown could well be construed as "Just A Dream". You can't go back, I'm sorry. I refute any defence that you read it in literature and demand that you quantify precisely how a million people every day turn on the television set and say "Testcard girl, testcard girl".

Obviously, Ms. Fletcher, if the assertion is spurious and disappears it doesn't matter, and if valid it would have to stay the same.

Yours, refraining from stating, "I Told You So",

Derek Philpott

Dear Derek,

Thanks for your query. However, your concerns as regards the claims in Testcard Girl are misplaced.

As you will be aware, the Testcard Girl appeared every day on BBC TV from 1967-98. Given that 30 million U.K. viewers watched a documentary about the Royal Family in 1969 and 32 million viewed Princess Diana's funeral in 1997, our estimate of one million people turning on the infinitely preferable and more ubiquitous Testcard Girl seems conservative!

It is not formally recorded how many of these people asked the Testcard Girl whether she was bored, but surely she must have been. She was sat there for 31 years with only a strange toy clown for a friend and without even finishing her game of noughts and crosses.

As such, I'm sure you'll agree that, far from being a creative allegorical exercise, the song Testcard Girl is pure documentary.

Thank you for your interest.

Amelia Fletcher

Ex-Talulah Gosh

Dear The ~~Ocean Outcasts~~ Sea Urchins,

Please don't cry, but "No Matter What" you may say about cackling cumuli, worried wobbly willows, pulsating petrified pines or frightened fluttery ferns out there in wild grass ~~pictures~~ pastures, I've been looking around again, The ~~Briny Beggars~~ Sea Urchins and it's "too hard I think" not to surmise that you are "wrong wrong".

I don't know if to let you down will put you in a
"Jam" The ~~Marine Mishiefs~~ Sea Urchins but I cannot
"open out" or "do all of the bending" of logic needed
to accommodate "clouds just laughing" and "Trees
shaking because they're scared again".

You can perhaps seek "Solace", The ~~Wave Wastrels~~ Sea
Urchins in Mr. Sting waffling on about the sun in
the envious sky or something.

Yours, looking "Day Into Day" for your response,

Derek Philpott

Dearest Derek,

Thanks for reaching out. If truth be told, the very occasional
fleeting contact regarding my former glories as one of the
iconic shambling janglers are all I live for any more. I sit,
Miss Havershamesque in my decaying anorak, waiting only
to be reminded of when the whole world seemed to turn on
just the merest waft of my polyester cravat.

Whilst my gratitude for your attention is undeniable, I feel I
must take issue with your apparent assertions that trees
cannot be frightened or indeed clouds enjoy a humorous
moment. Do you also doubt furious drizzle? Hysterical
shrubbery? Of course not. That would be plain silly.

I very much enjoyed your comedy alternative band names,
so much so I was positively smirking like the wind. The Sea
Urchins was in fact a last minute change to our initial
moniker. We were going to be called The Davy Jones
Locker Imps but the Sarah record label felt it was far too
sixties plus we were as scared as trees of being sued by
The Monkees who were all sporting very aggressive mullets
at that point in the 1980s. Talking of The Monkees, have
you by any chance written to last surviving member Micky
Dolenz and pulled him up on Porpoise songs? Thought not

you hypocrite.

Just off now to record our big comeback single (they're all doing it). It's called Macabre Barbara. Hope to hear from you again. Please.

James

The Sea Urchins

Dear The Orchids,

Re: Feline Felony

I'm ashamed to say that I could have been stupid for so long but we took our 6 week old tortoisehell - she's my girl - to a very busy local park last week.

It really is "A Kind Of Eden", although my nephew Dorian fell over under the bridge by a river and ended up with dirty clothing, leading us to declare, "this boy is a mess".

We were also plagued by some "Caveman" whose "Obsession No. 1", apart from to scare young people, was dobbing us in to the police for animal cruelty - at one point I feared I saw a "Blue Light". It's only obvious to those that "Defy The Law", so I was unaware that the coolest thing for little Bonnie was a place called home for the first five months.

Taking your lyrical advice, allowing a kitten to move through the crowd did not make him laugh out loud!

Hopefully, you know I'm fine and will "Hold-On" for your response, perhaps on a Sunday.

Yours, with "Apologies",

D Philpott

Dear Mr Philpott,

First, a big thank you and "Apologies" for the delay in responding to your letter. I've got a habit, or rather we have a habit, of being lazy... however, as you know, we have been striving, for years, for the lazy perfection.

Wow... you took your tortoiseshell to the park! Our cat Walter is nineteen and would never ever have allowed us to take him for a walk to the park. That's just something for the longing and until then you will find him on a lovely sheepskin rug underneath the window in a place called home sweet home. We used to take our last cat, Frank de Salvo, out in a pram for a walk all dressed up in doll's clothes. We would sometimes catch people looking and then get back the response, "sorry... I didn't mean to stare". We suppose we must have looked a bit strange though.

What a palaver for poor Dorian! That boy certainly was a mess. Hope he didn't hurt himself when he fell in the river. I imagine all you would have been able to do was just sigh and hope you weren't going to be in for another Long Drawn Sunday Night of laundry.

That sounds horrible to have been pestered by the caveman. He sounds like he was the true definition of a bastard. Can I recommend a trip down to the ocean, which might be a safer option for Bonnie and Dorian and one that will give them limitless joy? Just tell Dorian, "Take my Hand" and "turn your radio on" and next time he should stay safe and dry. Oh... and a picnic would be good. We were just dreaming there... lovely sandwiches, some peaches and remember to give a little honey on the side... it's so healthy and good for you. Bonnie might not like it though but she could have... now let's see... what could she have? That one has left us somewhat bemused, confused and bedraggled... Oh that's right... Bonnie could have some of those dreaming kind things that cats go daft for. Feel the magic Bonnie!

OMG… I should have thought it was not the wisest thing to do to take our lyrical advice. Thanks though for doing so. After all… we never thought we were clever but, hey, sometimes we do strike the right chord.

Mr D Philpott; we want you, we need you… to realise you have given us the craziest feeling in the warmest way with your very kind and good words (are never long).

Someone like you is good to know!

Doot doot for now,

The Orchids

Dear Razorcuts,

Re: Municipal Miscalculation

I hope you're satisfied, and "I'm sorry to embarrass you" but unless "there's something that I missed", "I have to raise" some Tall "Stor(e)yteller" concerns.

Dubai's Burj Khalifa, the world's largest skyscraper, stands at 829.8m (2,722ft), or just over half a mile. However, "I Heard You The First Time" today claiming to "walk beneath mile high towers", some 2,722ft in excess of said maximum peak.

You are undoubtedly sharp, Razorcuts, but it's "so hard finding something worth believing". Please prove yourselves "Brighter Now", and find a better way to explain this threadbare bridge of words. To avoid it is "too much like running away".

Yours, hoping your response will "Come My Way",

D Philpott

Dear Derek,

Thank you for writing to us. I wonder if you have considered the interesting question of precisely what we mean when we refer to the height of a structure. The observation in your letter is clearly based upon the assumption that a tower can only correctly be described as a "mile high" if the distance from its base to its summit is at least 5,280 feet. You have perhaps failed to take into account the possibility that a tower might be erected in a geographical location that is itself some distance above mean sea level. For example, Mexico City and Bogota in Columbia are both situated at an elevation of well over 7,000 feet, and it could therefore be argued that a very small tower in either of these cities would indeed be a mile high.

In fairness I must concede that, at the time I wrote the lyrics to the song, I possibly had in mind an office block in a less far-flung location, such as Southwark (where I worked at the time) or somewhere like Bootle or Telford. Admittedly, none of these places is located significantly above sea level. But the point still stands, I think.

You might be interested to know that it has been suggested that the term "mile high" in our song is in fact intended metaphorically, and relates to a particular mental state. It is likely that this would have caused the record to be banned from the airwaves had it been released in the Summer of Love. Just to be clear, I can confirm that as far as I'm aware no members of Razorcuts knowingly consumed dangerous or illegal chemicals. I did get very drunk on vodka and Irn Bru at a gig in Glasgow once, though.

Regards

Tim Vass, Razorcuts.

Dear Crazyhead,

Pedantry and pettiness can be such a tedious "grind" ~~Psychosupervisor~~ Crazyhead, making many "Pretty Sick". I'm normally "Above Those Things", but your infant receptacle refusal, "soon they may believe in Jesus... and that babies come from boxes", leads me to wonder if you are suffering from "Some Kinda Fever".

If I were to go "Out On A Limb", ~~Madmaster~~ Crazyhead, "I Can Do Anything" up to 100 examples to disprove your claim. However, I don't want that kind of love, so here are just six:-

Baby Type	Description of Box
Rosemary's	3 Disc (Blu-Ray) Collector's Edition Set
Bel	Cheese & Crackers Selection
Shark Cuddly Toy	Cardboard/See Through Plastic Container
Billion Dollar	Alice Cooper 40th Birthday 4 CD Package
Achtung	U2 40th Anniversary 4 x CD Package
Beanie	Perspex Protective Casing

I sincerely hope that these arguments do not inspire you to "Buy A Gun" and go "Bang Bang" in my general direction, and remain,

Yours sincerely,

D. Philpott

Dear Mr. Philpott,

Re: Your recent letter

Pedantry and pettiness? We believe we are "Above Those Things", and you don't need a "Fortune Teller" to tell you that! We may well be "fucked by rock", but you missed out "little" in ".and babies come from LITTLE boxes".

Perhaps you have been too long "In The Sun" with regard to your 6 baby types and boxes?

We could retort, "What Gives You The Idea You're So Amazing Baby?", but, then again, maybe you are a "Desert Orchid", flowering in a desert of retarded sexuality... or maybe that's us? A truly thoroughbred race winner? Have you been drinking baby turpentine, as that could certainly give you the runs? But hey, don't get that sinking feeling if it's just no rags to riches, just rags!

Life can be one long movie theme, but you can rub the Buddah or use your magic eye, Snakey-eyes.

You can say we can only give you everything, and don't get out on a limb, because everything's alright!

Dragster girl might smell like Fish, but no reason to walk the streets of Baltimore, or take a death ride to Osaka. We always consult our big sister in such manners, as she recites the ballad of baby turpentine.

Hoping to catch up with yourself, your partner in crime and also our old chum Norman Wisdom at the Screaming Apple so we can milk the badger!

Best wishes,

Crazyhead

P.S. As Winter approaches we may have long dark days, but if you keep away from Jack the Scissor Man and consult Cardinal Phink, shout "Here Comes Johnny", and don't play with matches... we don't want another tower of fire!

P.P.S. By the way Philpott; if not the Screaming Apple Nightclub with Norman, we suggest you look out each summer as Crazyhead have reformed in the last few years and usually play 5 or 6 gigs, so come on down.

Dear Mr Devant,

Perhaps "You Saw Me Coming", but I'm not even going to ~~try~~ attempt to fathom how those on your "Radar" with ginger hair, or, to employ the playground vernacular, "Duracells - with the copper top" are born out of time with the world behind them. You imply that this follicular minority historically prevailed over the "normal haired" in bygone days.

I concede that Columbus, Van Gogh, Oliver Cromwell, Galileo and Elizabeth the First's wig were all stricken with the contagion. It has now been inherited by Charlie Drake, Hucknall, Bianca off of Eastenders and Outspan in The Commitments. However, unless in a "Parallel Universe" there is no evidence to "open wider" the debate that carrot tops were the predominant tribe.

"I think about you", so feel that you should take a deep breath and tone down your "Swan Vesta Head" ode, renaming it, "You Must Be Burnt Sienna".

I now say "Goodnight", trusting that everything fits and you do not consider this missive "Out Of Order".

Wishing you and your apparitional other half well,

D Philpott

Dear Mr Philpott (& son),

Thank you for your recent letter. Your suggestion, therein, that we (David Devant and his Spirit Wife) alter the name of our song Ginger to Burnt Sienna is an intriguing one not least because I have a strong, personal affinity with the plight of the Italian City, from which the reddish brown pigment takes its name. This neurosis (I am comfortable describing it thus) derives from Sienna's battle with

the neighbouring republic of Florence as depicted
in the Rout of San Romano by Paulo Uccello 1440
(egg tempera with walnut oil and linseed oil on
poplar). Florence, as you may well know, considered
itself the seat of the scientific Renaissance as
embodied by the statue of David (devant Goliath –
Goliath not in shot). David is depicted in his 3-
metre state of undress caught in the act of
thinking. The intellect in this cognitive sense,
rather than being emblematic of an underdog, then
becomes the aggressor seeking to vanquish the more
'out of time' and metaphorically vague consciousness
of the Siennese society. The approximately six hour
rout of San Romano was won by the Florentine
cavalry though the Siennese would, in their heroic
vagueness declare it a victory for themselves, and
consequently the scientific paradigm of culture has
become the hegemonic state we now find ourselves in;
history being written by the victors. There is even
evidence to suggest that Leonardo da Vinci, the
great polymath of the republic of Florence, was
himself blessed with ringlets of a reddish brown
hue and it would also be logical to assume that his
open-minded and progressive curiosity would have
left him appalled at the thought of his joy of
wide-eyed creative entanglements being turned into
the dogma of scientific fixed-point perspective that
commands every cell of Western humanity today. I
cannot, therefore, fault the logic of your
nomenclature and subsequent requesting for the
alteration of this song's title. However, I am unable
to proceed with the appropriate logistical
activities until I receive assurance that any
pyrogenic damages to the person or property of one

Sienna Miller, a world renowned blonde-haired actress, will not be prosecuted as having been a result of our song's altered appellation. Many thanks for your interest in the songs and material of David Devant and his Spirit Wife and I hope you don't find my response too deflating or indeed in any way occluding of your genius for the retitling of lyrical beat pop.

Yours,

All done by kindness,

The Vessel

PS. I'm not altogether sure the song was meant to be about hair colour but found the subsequent publicity to be beneficial for the short-term promotion of the band's creative output.

Dear Ned's Atomic Dustbin,

Re: Deceased Appliance Confusion

According to the ad break in 'The Alan Titchmarsh Show', "washing machines live longer with Calgon". I fear that Calgon have made the same mistake as yourselves and Gary Numan, who also believes that electrical appliances display human characteristics.

On occasions such as 'Celebrity Love Island' and, indeed, 'The Alan Titchmarsh Show', it can be less than useful, but it is impossible, be it by throwing things or other means, and irrespective of whether the screen is 'plasma', to kill one's television.

Yours, through the usual 'channels',

D Philpott

Dear Mr Philpott,

You posit the impossibility of killing televisions, presumably in response to the exhortation in the lyrics of one of our better known pop lyrics, penned by someone we know simply as 'the singer'. In one sense, of course, you are perfectly right. Television is "a system for converting visual images (with sound) into electrical signals, transmitting them by radio or other means, and displaying them electronically on a screen". The device containing said screen is styled a "television receiving set" or, more usually in common speech, "a television" (definite article). Given that the most widely accepted definition of the verb 'to kill' is to "cause the death of a person, animal, or other living thing", we are clearly here dealing with the use of metaphor; something that lyricists are much inclined to pursue.

The lyric employs a third person narrative utilising passages of reported speech, describing a bad-tempered interlocution between a female protagonist and an unidentified second party with an objectionably poor understanding of an issue of some significance to our heroine.

The cause of the conflict seems to be the voicing of opinions by this second party, which are based not on first hand "lived" experience, but on the passive acceptance of information mediated through the television - possibly news media, but more likely popular drama, given the punning reference to "soap for sore eyes" later in the song.

The premise of the lyric is that the metaphorical killing of "your television" would force the protagonist's antagonist to engage in the real world and to confront their prejudices, formed through the unconscious and insidious accretion of opinions projected by mass media messaging.

Perhaps realising that the (possibly decades long)

accumulation of perspective cannot easily be rectified by the metaphorical extinction of the television, the woman/girl resorts instead to physicality and to the expulsion of the offender. Disoriented by this act of assertiveness, and 'falling about', the offender is displaced from, and replaced in, "her father's favourite chair" by the protagonist.

Will she succumb to the mind-numbing spoon feeding screen? Will she be seduced by power?

The television is not dead.

Yours,

Ned's Atomic Dustbin

Dear ~~Grenoble Guardians~~ Paris Angels,

I'm not a "Slippery Man", ~~Cherbourg Cherubs~~ Paris Angels, but of the "Purest Values", so unless I'm going round the bend again, I think I've got it all in hand.

I *think* I really understand, but if you could "Give Me More...Scope" and speak your desire as to which option is required to be displayed, this should lead me all the way and save you waiting an "Eternity", ~~Dieppe Divinities~~ Paris Angels.

Amongst others, ~~Saint-Denis Celestials~~ Paris Angels, there is the 43rd ranked British Prime Minister, a Cornwall Eco resort, or (perhaps "Too Easy"), a Biblical allotment.

"I understand" it's not easy coming down to one, ~~Versailles Visionaries~~ Paris Angels, but please take a look and tell me what "Show Me Eden" you find "to be higher" priority. Sorry to put it all on you, but "it's up to you baby!"

Yours,

D. Philpott

Dear Mr/Mrs Philpott,

Thank you for your enquiry/diatribe/musings.

Firstly, I'm ecstatic to confirm that it is not a thinly-veiled dig at Anthony Eden's handling of the Suez crisis that precipitated his resignation.

Secondly, even though it is a place where you can find Sundew plants, neither is it the Eden Project in Cornwall, soon to be thankfully in Morecambe too.

Thirdly, a common misconception, but one requiring further explanation; the song refers to the biblical Eden. We have had previous correspondence about this matter. This first arose in SwEDEN*, though when raised, prior engagements precluded us from defending ourselves in Stockholm (where there's fish in the sea and food on the shelves) so we sent our erstwhile stalwart defender Dinsdale. (*later cited as the Stockholm variation defence - ask a bishop).

The preposterous allegation was that Rikki was Adam and Jayne was Eve, singing in call and response. The lyrics that caused offence to those of a religious bent were: "(Rikki) Dance, let's see you dance ((Jayne) you are my world, my light, you are my God".

The outcome of this trial by/of super nature was just a mere simple misunderstanding - "Oh Yes" was a single released in 1991 on Virgin Records (not Virgin Mary Chain records) and of course 1991 was the year of Eden Hazard's birth, when we sang "show me Eden" - we were proclaiming the future herald of greatness - show us your mercurial talents with the orb of our religion, the football. Dance let's see you dance (with a ball at your feet).
Eternally Yours,

Lille Cherubim

Dear The Wolfhounds

<u>Re: The Anti-Midas Touch</u>

As a "Rule of Thumb", any element undergoing drastic alteration will change considerably, The Wolfhounds. I'm therefore not "Blown Away" by your assertion, "you're just not the same when I turn you to gold".

Furthermore, as I have not personally suffered the aforementioned alchemical transformation, I am "torn in two" by a declaration which can only be concluded to be "Disinformation".

However, my wife is "hell bent" on not putting "One Foot Wrong" perfecting a Shepherd's Pie as we speak, so I agree that I am "in love with the girl who works in my kitchen".

Yours, trusting that I "See You Reply" soon,

D Philpott

Dear D Philpott,

It's pointless killing me when your living fossil attitude borders on cruelty. You put forward the wrong foot one day and, subsequently, you are unable to make people invisible. Do you get my drift? Would like to think so. If you think dead, the corpse deflates to the ground and dies the small death. Goodbye laughter, hello side effects.

We slide like rats on a raft, tomorrow attacking each restless spell. Every day, monsters in transit cheer up the hall of mirrors. Everybody's traveling; abstract, hopeful, feeling so strange again, yet, blown away. The tools of the dark have obsolescence built in, so much so that one sees nothing of the sun from one miserable summer to the next. It's gutter charity. Look at Spotify playlists for proof of that. The middle-aged freak to a non-specific song they rent. Act the ten commandments of public life, sure, but divide and fall?

Just like magic triggers the comedian's feeding frenzy, sandy natural disasters recycle security, yet still can't see the light. I'm a killer whale on the beach. The dead sea burning opposite land across the river of death. Apparition: I see you!

The devil looks after her own skyscrapers, but neither vertical grave nor tunnel stand apart. No rite of passage is personal when you sing the song of the Afghan shopkeeper. You blew nowhere, but I ask you, lost but happy shopper, are you feeling lucky? Heather? Celeste? It's called progress, Cath.

It was extremely handy Howard's fire in the home was not torture. Lightning's going to strike again, but as a rule of thumb, rain stops play. No soap in a dirty war will cleanse the roaches, but the stupid pour cocktails with names like Blue Nowhere and Midget Horror whilst off their skull: face down in a mess of paradise.

Like most people, we don't believe anything, and I have never been unable to transform cryptic disinformation into anything that resembles anything related, or indeed, useless.

I always come second, my cousin. I have what is known as the Andy Midas touch.

After all, you must remember that these are just the words of a single God Led Warning.

Thanks

Wolfhounds (No 'The'. Lazy, eh?)

PS ... and Electric Music

Dear Senseless Things,

I have a friend, ~~Out Cold Artifacts~~ Senseless Things, named Andy Carman. I'd never bother being part of it myself but he often likes to "Come Together" with a coachful to the Mecca in Salisbury.

On a comfort break, despite protests that they "Can't Do Anything" and were "Splitting Hairs", he was issued with an on the spot fine for knocking back three cans of Stella at the Pay & Display.

I accept that the common pilsner is "No Substitute" for the upmarket cocktail, but "Is It Too Late" to ask if you were similarly penalised for leaning on a parking meter sipping on a margarita?

I hope, ~~Comatose Commodities~~ Senseless Things, that you ignore your primary instinct to "see red" at my appearing "Too Much Like I Know You". As an aside, congratulations on being personally namechecked, via Mr. Bowie, by a continuous sequence of events in the offstage area of a theatre.

Yours,

D. Philpott

Dear Mr D. Philpott,

Firstly, as a concerned reader, please increase the dosage of medication. You're clearly having *another wobble*. (Let's hope it doesn't escalate to the point where you're burying your pants in the garden again). You seem to be referencing song titles and lyrics in your obsessional manner as per last time, focusing in on tiny details and reading hidden meanings into simplistic song titles. These are the warning signs, remember? I could equally (and nonsensically) ask you, Mr D - exactly which Pott did you choose to Phil?

Listen - you need to lean into the friendship you have with

Andy here. Although given his predilection for cans of Stella, you best catch him early before he's started off on the lager again.

I spoke to Brendan from Teenage Fanclub the other day. He said that he's also received one of your surreal harassments. He strongly ensures he was only a *fan of teenagers* when he was himself a teenager, and is at pains to clarify - he no longer writes to any of them anymore.

No. I don't believe any fine was incurred for the parking meter incident. The said tequila had only impaired the ability to stand up straight, and not create a dilution of any particular moral code or socially acceptable conduct.

Again - the obsessional quest to uncover hidden meanings in obscure lyrics and imagined references - there is no oblique strategy at play here. No *Enigma Code* to crack. (Of course I would say that, though, wouldn't I? To throw you off the scent.) But you do rapidly appear to be turning into the Alan Turing of the Indie Pop-Rock world. I must ask - is the acid very strong round your parts? Or did you sample the Cornish Brown batch? I told you to steer well clear of that. No good can come of this pursuit. Not for someone in current & gainful employment as a Nonsense Farmer.

Yours sincerely,

Cass Browne,
13th Tentacle of The Black Squid Zodiac.

P.S. In regards to your last point, which I can only assume is referencing the lyrics to the song "Time" by Mr. David Bowie. As Mr. David says - "Time" does indeed "speak of Senseless Things". His script is me and you. To reassure you further though, fortunately, none of the members of any of these aforementioned groups have ever fallen *wanking to the floor*. I hope this clears up your last point.

Dear The June Brides,

If you are "Waiting For A Change", please do take "Comfort" from what could be "The Instrumental" cure for your "revolutionary" insomnia.

From Saturday to Sunday, the remedy is "just the same", The ~~Solstice Spouses~~ June Brides.

Rather than nocturnal laps of the bedroom or inexplicable slumber spins, may I instead suggest merely remaining static and counting sheep or, if, "There Are Eight Million Stories…", seeing how many of those you can get through before dropping off.

You may be surprised at "What Time Can Do", and hopefully will no longer feel the need to go round in circles as you go to sleep at night.

I look forward to hearing from you within three days, unless of course "I Fall" asleep myself.

Yours,

D Philpott

Dear Mr Philpott,

Thank you for your recent letter. As you can probably guess, we do get some very odd missives, so it's somewhat of a relief to receive a relatively straightforward one.

As I understand it, you appear to suggest that listening to our music is an excellent aid to a good night's sleep. This comes as something of a surprise, as we had laboured, for several years, under the illusion that our music might, in some way, act in quite the opposite manner - inducing something approaching wakefulness, if not an entirely positive mood. We appear to have been mistaken, and are very grateful to you for having bought this to our attention.

One of the group has suggested, in the light of your suggestion, that future concerts could perhaps involve camp beds, essential oils and low-dash level lighting to further enhance the feeling of slumber - with possible audience somnambulance to follow. Sleepwalking dancers would be a rare treat to behold!

Should we successfully pursue this option, and financial success follows our new-found stylings, then rest assured that you will be fondly remembered, if not necessarily financially recompensed.

Yours etc.

Phil Wilson, The June Brides

Dear The Jasmine Minks,

I discovered you whilst mistakenly googling, "Can I put skimmed mink in Jasmine Tea?". After "I gladly placed my trust in you", I ended up "Black and Blue" - your equation with radiance and agility literally "Cut Me Deep" on a Saturday afternoon!

After months of asking, "Summer! Where?", I ventured "Step By Step" into my garden in blazing sunshine, marvelling at Mother Nature. Banishing bad thoughts behind me, and thinking "Nothing Can Stop Me", I gave myself a thirty second set up and began "Running Ahead" at my eight foot high lattice fence.

"We're Up High… It's Time To Win", I thought, expecting to vault it.. but I went into freefall, landing face first onto my shiny and black tarmac.

I must now "Learn To Suffer" lacerations, never again believing you assert that I can "clear massive hurdles since you delivered me into the light".

Yours, wishing it would rain,

D Philpott

Dear Mr. Philpott,

It's a bit unsettling to think that after all these years someone can still chance upon the name Jasmine Minks. The name comes from a cabal of revolutionaries in north-east Scotland who lived in Jasmine Terrace (Jasmine was pronounced Jas, like glass and mine like coal mine). The 'mink' part comes from an Aberdeen word which means a poor or raggedly-dressed person. The name was code for those who opposed the tyrannical capitalist system!

The name was meant to have been expunged years ago. I am assuming that somewhere in the dark web the secret is still going? You seem to have found the portal. Our mission was top secret but in the mists of time I suppose I can tell our true story and our alter-ego as a pop group. Our name should have been airbrushed from history much like Trotsky from Stalin-era photographs. We should have been obliterated from any mark on photos, biographies and mentions on the internet. Unfortunately the world is changing and we no longer have faith in the puppets who run the world from the USA to China and Russia and so the bureaucracy is getting careless and things slip. The will is there no more. Dictators ain't what they used to be!

Your attempt at escape, vaulting over the lattice fence, was admirable. But stupid. It reminded me of our time with the Stasi in East Germany. We went to Berlin as a pop group and card-carrying members of the Young Communist Party (GB). We were easy pickings, ready to be indoctrinated. We saw first hand the machine which kept its citizens in line. A show was made of anyone trying to scale the wall. In reality they could walk through the Brandenburg Gate with a pass to work in the west of the city. Our task was to infiltrate the left-leaning indie pop market in the UK and recruit for the 5th International, the creation of a super revolutionary party worthy of leading the world into the next socialist epoch.

The Times (Ed Ball mysteriously had a group of the same name!) were changing and after the Berlin Wall came down we lost our contacts and financial backing as a group. Thatcherism became too strong for us and wooed us into submission as we declined into toothless, blubbering idiots high on whatever we could find on the streets.

We had some successes but the party became more of a drink 'n' drugs party as we became addicted to mind-altering substances rather than social-altering politics. We hid it well though and our great leader, Comrade McGee, even managed to infiltrate the UK government and act as a double agent. But all to no avail, as even him exaggerating the supposed weapons of mass destruction lie and the subsequent invasion by western armies in the Middle East proved.

It was supposed to be a catalyst for the masses to rise and overthrow their capitalist oppressors - it actually backfired and had the opposite effect of cementing the oil barons' power.

So Mr. Philpott, the world has changed; borders constantly moving, new countries being dissolved, others created or re-created. Is it time for a Jasmine Minks reinvention?

Yours,

Jim Shepherd

Dear ~~Jumpy Jerk~~ Nervous Twitch,

I've just been to the dentist. A crown fell off a few months ago, but I knew that Mr. Gittings could "Put Me Back Together". He complained that I "Should've Come By" much sooner, and then administered a local anaesthetic and started "Messing With My Head".

"Even Though I Have Regrets", it did "Torment Me", and I left "Tongue Tied" with my mouth "Numb".

There was "Something Wrong With Me", and, fearing "Another Fight", I phoned First Direct expressing my "Boredom And Dissatisfaction" at their failure to cancel my Netflix Direct Debit. I "Soon Found Out" that this was a mistake; the Lidocaine hadn't worn off, and there was a crackle throughout the call.

It was agreed, ~~Edgy Spasm~~ Nervous Twitch, that I'd ring back, "and we did" speak immediately as I didn't have to "Get Back In Line" in a queue. This time, when asked if I could hear her properly I replied "Clear as a bell" which sadly came out as "Clarabella'.'

I therefore put it to you, ~~Tense Twinge~~ Nervous Twitch, that your fella who you heard on the phone talking to 'Clarabella' may not be "Oh-so Keen" on infidelity but instead may similarly have failed to exercise "A Little Self Discipline", and contacted his bank too soon after having a molar capped.

"I Won't Hide" stating that your response is "Something To Look Forward To".

Yours, hoping not to be seen as "That Weird Guy",

D Philpott

Dear D Philpott,

I read your letter after waking from a terrible *TARANTINO HANGOVER*. (For those that are unaware, this is when your memories of the night before are jumbled up and not in the order of the actual time line of events, and appear a bit crazy, like a Tarantino film!). *WHAT THE HELL* is this all about I thought to myself. Not wanting to *WASTE MY TIME* I quickly put pen to paper to respond. Here at Twitch HQ we'd hate for you to think that *WE DON'T CARE*!

I guess regardless of your tooth twangs *SOME PEOPLE NEVER CHANGE*, and with your *BAD REPUTATION* I know that we *SHOULD'VE COME BY* to assist with your credit card crisis. But you really should *FORGIVE YOURSELF*; I'm sure the staff at First Direct frequently tell themselves *NOT EVERYONE'S OUT TO GET ME*.

We don't want to have the *LAST LAUGH* here but who has Netflix these days anyway? Everyone knows the best stuff is on Disney!

On the subject of my fella, *ANOTHER WAY* I see it is that he had just stolen that girl Clarabella in the first place, right out of a Beatles song, probably because *SHE'S SO HIP*. But I'm not going to admit *THE WAY THAT I FEEL* on the situation, as you can't be *THIS MAD AT THE WORLD* for too long.

But I can reassure you that *IT'S GOING TO BE OK* with your foul fangs, and if it gets bad again make sure your dentist gives you *MORE THAN ENOUGH WARNING* before your actions *SNOWBALL* into another call centre catastrophe. *BUT DON'T BLAME* me if it does happen, or at least, just *DON'T BE MEAN* to more minimum wage workers!

Erin

Dear Silvery,

I chanced upon your output whilst searching for discount imitation precious metal bracelets online.

Whilst your sound 'Sparks' enthusiasm, I feel that the subject matter of your lyrics may give potentially interested 'A & R' people horrors (horrors, horrors).

Amongst all the UFOs in graveyards and Victorian Martians pilfering pets nonsense, I was given hope by "The Naked And The Dead" and "An Account Of The Raising Of A Spirit"... before realising that they're not about a gangster hit in a Jacuzzi or hoisting a Dirty Martini aloft in a trendy nightclub.

Finally, you may be scuppered by potential audiences thinking you're a Blondie tribute band accounting for Deborah Harry's current follicular hue.

I hope that my interpretation of that which is and that which is not does not offend, and remain,

Yours, sincerely scrutinising the devil in the detail,

D. Philpott

Dear Mr Philpott,

Many thanks for your recent letter. I can see where the confusion would've started thinking that Silvery was some kind of dodgy online jeweller! It's the name! But I can assure you that with the money I made from record sales and live engagements over the years I have no need to dabble in any kind of dubious moneymaking schemes. An absolutely ridiculous notion. The magnificence of our whole worldview changed so many fundamental laws of the way rock and pop was thought about in our late Noughties heyday that to think that we were not justly rewarded financially is preposterous. An absolute insult to our art.

Just out of interest though mate, what exactly were you after? I happen to have a few lovely necklaces just in. Rings more your thing? Well just let me know because I'm seeing a pal this weekend who can sort you out. Lovely stuff. Really nice. Looks great and pretty weighty. Top quality silverish metal at low low prices. Bracelets you say? No worries.. with a few days' notice I can get it. If you need any unsold Silvery records too, I've got boxes. Literally boxes of the things.

Full catalogue enclosed with reply.

Yours

James Orman

(Silvery Traders)

Dear Boo Hewerdine,

Re: NHS Television Programme Controversy

Mr. Robert Williams has very vocally proclaimed his preference towards this gritty hospital drama over its rivals Holby City, Casualty and the particularly poorly acted '24 Hours in A&E'.

I hope therefore that you "know there's something wrong" in subjecting fictional poorly people to the judicial system.

To "try the patients of Angels" is just not on, Mr Hewerdine, especially considering that in 'real life' many of these 'background artists' are themselves between jobs with only "a little money saved".

Yours, anticipating to be waiting until I die,

D Philpott

Dear Mrs Pillpop,

It is in my nature to be judgemental. And, having once reached my biased verdict, to dispense disproportionately punitive justice. I am, in short, a bigot. I come from a long line of bigots. In fact, my great-grandfather was the County bigot of Lincolnshire. So narrow-minded and one-sided was he that he was briefly considered for the position of Lord Bigot Of London. Sadly, on the morning of his possible selection he was heard to mutter the words, "you may have a point there", and was immediately disqualified.

Being a bigot is not as easy as you might think. It can be a lonely life fraught with irrational bile. I can, at any moment, take terrible umbrage at the slightest deviation from my outlandish views. I once managed to take offence at my own reflection. My first word was a tut. That said, I have a placard made from a whiteboard so that I can change my mind at a moment's notice. For, you see, Mrs P, I am that rare creature; a capricious bigot. The target of my ire may one minute be astro-turf and the next, people of average height. I wake every morning in a state of high dudgeon in a fever of irrational anger. I roam my house roaring in unfocused rage. Sometimes, when at a loose end, I will go to the park and hurl abuse at the swans. And yet two days later I may be back there serenading the same birds with my travel lute. As you can imagine, the cocktail of bigotry and indecision makes my life rather challenging. The bottom line is, although I feel very strongly about the content of your letter, I'm not exactly sure if I am in agreement or deeply offended. Am I for you or against you? Do you make salient points or do I feel like yelling that you have diarrhoea for brains? Only time will tell. Thank you for your interest.

B Hewerdine

Dear The Telescopes,

With "Precious Little" time to spare, it was "Everso" frustrating dropping my friend off at the North Riding bus station yesterday, to be quite honest.

My patience was threadbare as I witnessed a young female sauntering across the pedestrian crossing's "lines and space", engrossed in her mobile phone. She was looking neither "over here or over there", and "Anticipating Nowhere" near the level of road safety required, "as (I saw) the Light Return" to green. "Something In My Brain" told me I'd never get Gerald in a ~~catholic~~ Catterick shelter in time, and a "Pulsing Bead" of sweat ran "Down On Me" face.

I obviously saw no need for "Violence" and mumbled "I'd Never Hurt You", but something in my system somewhere, but I don't know what, sympathised with your desire "to kill a slow girl walking".

Your Hubble Servant,

D. XXXXXX A.K.A. Philpott
Stonehenge

Dear AKA Philpott,

Subject: 4,000 years Of Sunrises

Where Do We Begin? To Kill A zebra crossing? Come Bring Your Love my friend. You're Never Alone With Despair but We See Magic where we can don't we? It's lovely to hear you're from the stones; can you hear them listening? From The Inner Void I Fear they're speaking. You should tape it forever Now or at least find A Good Place To Hide; A Cabin In The Sky? Down By The Sea maybe? Or under Another Sky? I could set up my Psychic Viewfinder If You Can Not Be Sure... but There Is No Floor, This Train WILL keep on rolling but we are so Threadbare.

Strange Waves going around these days AKA Philpott, it's a Tidal Bandwidth. If You Can't Reach What You Hunger I would question everything. You Know The Way I'm sure. Living is dreaming of living but This Is Not A Dream.

Anyway, You Were Never Here if in doubt.

Wish Of You.

Stephen Lawrie

From The Telescopes (not The Telescopes' People)

*Prior to agreeing to correspond, The Telescopes insisted on the following conditions, which were complied with:-

"As you may imagine we receive an overwhelming amount of greetings from people of all walks of life who profess their proposed greetings are of Stonehenge origin.

For verification purposes, please send all correspondence as a series of picture postcards conveying the town in question. Please note, all written communication must be dispatched by Royal Mail, first class, with an authentic Stonehenge postmark to the following location: (ADDRESS CENSORED)"

Dear Big Flame,

I "warmed" to you while researching Zippo lighters, and am impressed that your famous rock and roller boogie inability thesis has been acted upon by Genesis (who have now admitted that they can't do it).

However, elsewhere within "Why Popstars Can't Dance", ~~Brilliant Blaze~~ Big Flame, you 'grass up' Sally, whose obsession with a diminutive French megalomaniac leads to her brandishing a large cutlass and slaying male children.

I don't believe it, not even for a minute, ~~Considerable Conflagration~~ Big Flame. If, as you claim, she wears a sword like Napoleon and she kills the boys, I'm pretty sure that Channel 5 would have made a documentary about it by now!

Yours in anticipation, and no ~~Enormous Inferno~~ Big Flame, I can't wait till next week!

Yours,

Derek Philpott

Dear Derek Philpott

What the Jazz-Fuck are you on about?

You are clearly not a man of few syllables - more a cat with cholic who collaborates in tune with the economic gloom. We were the breath of a nation yet you sink so low as to accuse us of wanting to re-write the American Constitution with our cubist pop manifesto, whereas we were more concerned in ensuring that all the Irish must go to heaven rather than ¡¡Cuba!!

To you it must seem like a new way, or even a quick wash and brush up with Liberation Theology, but there are millions like us 3 on baffled island who find your hard rock movement wears our Carol out and sometimes gives her the illness so bad that she gets earsore. She then bangs on to Debra about the Sargasso sea where the eels come from - managing this is very tough and if you don't have rigour and rhythmic feet then you have every chance of falling over purses and tripping over gold discs, no matter how hard you try not to.

Anyway, you've got the wrong band - we were bIG fLAME, not "Big Flame", so you WILL have to wait 'til next week.

Also, our lawyers will be in touch regarding your outrageous claims of why popstars can't dance - a complete disregard for the English Channel samba that clearly states "you'll never see a model sweat" - ain't it just so?

In the meantime, we suggest you turn your fear into dynamism, and refuse to believe in the biggest lie. Make sure you substitute invention for that unit-shifting pout, and let beauty be your future, as you get paraded down the golden aisle.

In short, go *XPQWRTZ* yourself.

Kind regards,

bIG fLAME

Dear ~~The Titian Trio~~ 3 Colours Red,

I'm not one of those "Paranoid People" that believes artists in the music business and anyone "who wants to live in Hollywood" are ancient lizards, ~~Crimson Clusters~~ 3 Colours Red, although there is arguably many a "Counterfeit Jesus".

Given therefore that to have done so would make you at least 2,739 years old, ~~Vermilion Varieties~~ 3 Colours Red, it'll be some time "Til I'm Ready" to believe that you've been "down here a million days".

As for the "Age of Madness", I've just heard their "Song On The Radio" and in the "Repeat To Fade" the DJ did "Say Something" about Suggs being 62, but I'm suffering "Mental Blocks" about the rest of them.

Yours, hoping not to receive a "Fake Apology",

D Philpott

Dear Mr Philpott,

I'm not sure where you got my address or the *Nerve (Gas)* to drop me a line, but I have to say that your missive sent me into quite the *Pirouette*.

Anyway, I've just returned from a *(Nuclear) Holiday* in Sussex (camped *Halfway Up The Downs*, in fact), where every day was a *Beautiful Day*. Having just got *Back To The City*, I'm not really in the mood to deal with obscure theories about whether myself and my erstwhile compatriots in *Rock* in fact have reptile DNA or are *Pure* products of the *Human Factory*.

As for your speculation about the age and longevity of a certain ska revival group, I think you need to be careful not to *Paralyse* your faculties *Calling To The Outside* of the realms of sanity. Take an *Intermission*, suck an *Aniseed* ball, *Desensitise* yourself, sing yourself a *Lullaby* and before you know it, *The World Is Yours*.

Let's call a *Ceasefire*.

Yours,

Ben Harding,

3 Colours Red
(Mark 1)

Dear These ~~Beast Blokes~~ Animal Men,

I "Know It's Hard" having your claim that "You're Always Right" challenged, but Homo Sapiens and, "by extension", builders, weren't around in The Jurassic Period. They were therefore unable to secure "Jobs For The Boys", so I cannot reconcile the construction of "High Riser" partitions.

As for the impossibility of Diplodocus dexterity with a plumb line and Brontosaurus bricklaying, it was never a question of lying and all of this news is probably obvious.

Admittedly, "We Are Living" in an era of Creationism, These ~~Quadruped Geezers~~ Animal Men, but to state, "like a dinosaur she's goin' off the wall" is an argument fairly easy to SMASH.

Yours, hoping that you do not feel "Too Sussed",

Derek Philpott

Dear Derek Philpott,

Yabba dabba (Ya) do have a point Mr. Derek re: these impossible 'oxy'morons. Position 'You're Always Right' and see also 'You're Always So Self Righteous' for context immediately after you've said it.

Re: builders in pre-hysterical times: Were we really?...

...Or were we sweet knuckle-dragging dreamers lost in wonder at an ideal hovel exhibition searching for the new cave of the (yeah you can guess it).

Yes, the 90s when monsters ruled the earth and little these ant men tried not to get too squashed or gassed - as you know those herbivore tree top munchers really could pack a punch....Good lord!

Let's talk Creationism. Or not. It's up to you.

...'like a dinosaur she's going off the wall' said Karl Marks just before he opened his first food and clothing retail store and I think we can all see his point.

Are *you* feeling 'Too Sussed'?... Is sussed a feeling? Or a state of divine smugness, a vain glorious futile bauble.

Hey all meander'tholls.

Is there a better way to spend your time?

Being fairly easily SMASHED has been an absolute gift.

Thanks for bringing it up.

But hey! Let's not make a song and dance about it.

These Animal Men

Dear S*M*A*S*H,

I am outraged by "Lady Love Your ****".

"I Thought I Was Right", but checked the Trading Standards Act. Silk Cut and its ilk can't be sold seperately, as this would bypass the Government Health Warning that they may "Kill Somebody". I feel incandescent. This image should be ever present.

No matter how much he may cry (or "Turn On The Water" works), the proprietor concerned has him"self abused" the right to operate an Off Licence, and may now be banned for up to "15 years".

Even though his position as a tobacconist could be compromised, please therefore provide details of the retailer from whom you can "go get a cigarette because he sells singles over there but he's not open yet". He must be taught a very, very valuable lesson.

Yours, hoping not to wait for the "Rest Of My Life",

D Philpott

Dear Mr D Philpott,

Shame on you. You pompous, overfamiliar, know-all Small Town Git.

Lady Love Your C*** is, was and will always be a love song, a fighting song, an anti-establishment song.

The Lady at Kings Cross did not smoke Silk Cut - she smoked Marlboro reds, or Bensons or Gitanes perhaps! - a French kiss.

Clearly you are confused in an 'Eats shoots and leaves' sort of way...

So...........

"Babe let's go get a cigarette, I know a man who sells singles over there". **"Fags and Wax"** - cigarettes and vinyl; an interesting retail experience. Didn't catch on like Cigarettes and Alcohol but hey! It seemed like a good idea at the time.

So, no Mr Philpott, you are not Right we are Left. We are all that is left after everyone has Killed Somebody.

Yours effervescently.

SMASH

Dear The ~~Joyous Junctions~~ Brilliant Corners,

Everything I ever wanted from our politicians, The ~~Remarkable Right Angles~~ Brilliant Corners, was to know that "Somebody Up There Likes Me", not grow cold, aware that they've got a "Long Long Way To Go".

The present government of over sixteen years is tipped to suffer "A Very Easy Death" in the next Election, The ~~Cracking Crannies~~ Brilliant Corners, and the funniest thing about it being caught so many times with its pants around its ankles is that "Brian Rix" could be rebooted as "It's just you remind me of The Conservative Party... When you pull down your trousers it sends me in fits".

Trust me, "You Don't Know How Lucky You Are", ~~The Top Notch Nooks~~ Brilliant Corners, to have the chance to illicit a "Big Hip" Hip Hooray from the populace. "Please Please Please" get it up to the recording studio and get it down on tape!

Yours, hoping to hear back one of these days,

D Philpott

Dear ~~Flowerpot~~ Philpott,

Any association with the Conservative Party would leave me 'Tangled up in Blue'. They always say 'Trust Me', then 'I Never Said That'. If I had 'A Rope In My Hand' I know what I'd do with it!

Your suggestion to reboot 'Brian Rix' is apt, particularly as Boris Johnson has been caught with his pants down on numerous occasions! 'Laugh I Could Have Cried'; he's about 'As Subtle As The Bomb'. We're all relieved he's 'Gone'; however you never know what's 'Around the Bend ' with the Tories.

BTW your letter seems to be full of my song titles? Or is this 'Egotistical Me' 'Delirious' and deluded?

I might go back in the Studio or do 'Nothing'.

Anyways, thanks for getting in touch.

"With A Kiss",

Davey

Dear Bis,

<u>Re: The Secret Vampire Soundtrack</u>

We discovered you because the parquet floor that we paid £1300 for from 'Wood I Lie' is peeling, and we're trying to locate other victims of "Fraudulent D.I.Y.".

"Protection" of a clandestine coven collective was not best sustained by releasing a record about it. 1,000s of shopaholics (85 in today's terms) *did* "listen up" when it reached number 47 in the hit parade in 1996.

The end starts today, Bis. What you're afraid of – exposure of your secret succubus society, and the resultant action and drama, can be avoided by:

a) Deleting the confession in all formats: 7 and 12 inch vinyl, cassette, CD, and personalised limited edition with a nice little sticker and Metal Box.

b) Obscuring these puncture marks that you're trying to hide by wearing a tasteful roll-neck jumper.

c) As a film states, "Do NOT talk about Vampire Club".

I was going to question the reality of demonic bloodsuckers but remembered that I've got to do my Self-Assessment by January 31st or be fined by HMRC. I've never met them but I can't forget them.

Yours,

D. Philpott

Dear Mr Philpott,

Firstly, we thank you for getting in touch as transmissions on this tip are infrequent at best these days. If you have experienced any "Slight Disconnects" in your parquet flooring then please do "Return To Central" immediately.

Please do not shabbily package to pretend that you are cool; we have your personal number and will be in touch should this be the case.

Your insinuation of any covert activity from our team is something we take seriously, but to paraphrase a famous advertising slogan, here at Bis, we give you "Exactly what it says on the Rin".

Surely there can be no clearer caveat emptor than "This Is Fake D.I.Y". Unfortunately, you have purchased in anticipation of some hidden meaning about the state of the music business, when all you have done is shelled out on substandard wares despite extremely visible warnings. Our other operations, "Kandy Pop" and "Sweet Shop Avengerz" are not, as many would have you believe, barbed metaphors about the collapse of small local industry and the brutal victory of capitalism, but are in fact childish odes to confectionary. Whilst our own uncovering of our shadowy bloodthirsty hobby may have its contradictions, the consistency here is that Bis always hide in plain sight. At least until Midnight on a daily basis.

We hope this experience hasn't put you off using our services in future. Perhaps you may wish to upgrade your home radio set-up by contacting "The New Transistor Heroes" or have some electrical issues that could be solved by our "Starbright Boy"?

If you'd like a full visual presentation of the services we provide, we can book you an appointment with our PowerPoint Girls.

Yours,

Bis

Dear Mr Wylie off of Cosmic Rough Riders,

The local Freemasons, who obviously care little for the "Value of Life" when it comes to pigs, recently held an 11am August Bank Holiday Hog Roast in their very own "Garden of Eden" – The Worshipful Master's spacious back patio in Devizes.

The fundraising event saw all '"Brothers Gather Round" the grill in the morning sun, enjoying the "Country Life", but sadly the rotisserie motor jammed, and the pork was only cooked on one side with the rest of it raw, ~~Stellar Sailors~~ Cosmic Rough Riders.

Needless to say, all of the ungrateful Lodge members felt "The Pain Inside" when they got "Back Home Again", no doubt fully refuting your statement, "We don't need a revolution in the summertime".

Yours, hoping to hear, yeah today, or any other day,

D. Philpott

Dear Derek,

The next time you write to me, please put a bloody stamp on the envelope, as I had to pay postage to read your letter.

At the time of writing this, I am an ancient, decrepit 64 year old man. A has-been who never really was, with a dodgy hip and a shaky knee. However, I still have all my own teeth and they're in very good condition, considering they've bitten off more than I could possibly ever chew.

I donated the excess to the poor.

I never did find out what happened to that young, uniformed chap in the park who tried his damndest to recruit me to the British Army on that warm summer's day.

I told him bluntly that we didn't need a Revolution, that we should enjoy the beer, the pretty girls and the glorious sunshine of the day. Alas, I fear it was too little too late as he'd obviously already been brainwashed.

Chances are, he had had his limbs detached from his torso while fighting a senseless War in The Falklands.

As for those darned Freemasons, they are pluralising and can be found in the strangest of places. Some are even now working as Football Referees in the Scottish Premier League, where they are well-known for their dodgy handshakes and biased decisions helping out their favourite team, Rangers.

From one wise old Walrus to another...

Adios.

DW.

Dear The Chefs,

Someone I know states that your combined podiatic protection and fashion advice should not be one of "these things you are proud of".

Georgie "Bloomers" Bloomfield, a highway maintenance engineer, heard you "Boasting" of ultra-all-seasons-durability footwear equally adaptable to "One Fine Day" and many rotten ones, so he bought a pair. Attending a flooded pothole on the A23, he slipped into what labourers technically term 'Road Bisto', and suffered a sodden instep – the puddle penetrated the near-plimsoll's flimsy hemp substitute.

He was therefore much louder than normal when protesting that the pair of canvas shoes that you have are *not* "just the thing in any kind of weather"!

Please apologise to Georgie, "Strictly" within "24 Hours" in order that we may let sleeping dogs lie!

Yours,

D. Philpott

Dear Mr/Mrs/Ms Philpott and Mr/Mrs/Ms Bloomfield,

Thank you for your letter.

It is always exciting to hear from people who listen to our songs, even if they do so with the wrong sort of ears.

Maybe if you understood that we are not a load of cobblers, but are in fact a cobbled-together group of would-be musicians, that might help with your predicament.

In the same way that you would not expect shoe manufacturers and retailers to be able to cook up and serve a three-course dinner with any sort of competence, you should not expect Chefs to supply you with reliable footwear, even if we pretend we can.

I don't want to get into an argument about this.

'Let's Make Up'.

Best wishes,

Helen McCookerybook

Dear ~~Mormon State Martyrs~~ Utah Saints,

To put it in three simple words, "How, Utah Saints", did you coerce Kate Bush, Annie Lennox, Mr. Oakey off of The Human League and all the others into a Band Aid-like scenario whereby they converged upon your Salt Lake studios and sang the same things again and again, over your loud "electronica beats"?

Yours, in "Lost Vagueness",

D Philpott

Dear Mr Philpott,

U-U-U-Utah Saints! U-U-U-Utah Saints!

U-U-U-Utah Saints! U-U-U-Utah Saints! U-U-U-Utah Saints!
U-U-U-Utah Saints! U-U-U-Utah Saints! U-U-U-Utah Saints!
U-U-U-Utah Saints! U-U-U-Utah Saints! U-U-U-Utah Saints!
U-U-U-Utah Saints! U-U-U-Utah Saints! U-U-U-Utah Saints!
U-U-U-Utah Saints! U-U-U-Utah Saints! U-U-U-Utah Saints!
U-U-U-Utah Saints! U-U-U-Utah Saints! U-U-U-Utah Saints!
U-U-U-Utah Saints! U-U-U-Utah Saints! U-U-U-Utah Saints!
U-U-U-Utah Saints! U-U-U-Utah Saints! U-U-U-Utah Saints!
U-U-U-Utah Saints! U-U-U-Utah Saints! U-U-U-Utah Saints!
U-U-U-Utah Saints! U-U-U-Utah Saints! U-U-U-Utah Saints!
U-U-U-Utah Saints! U-U-U-Utah Saints! U-U-U-Utah Saints!
U-U-U-Utah Saints! U-U-U-Utah Saints! U-U-U-Utah Saints!
U-U-U-Utah Saints! U-U-U-Utah Saints! U-U-U-Utah Saints!
U-U-U-Utah Saints! U-U-U-Utah Saints! U-U-U-Utah Saints!
U-U-U-Utah Saints! U-U-U-Utah Saints! U-U-U-Utah Saints!
U-U-U-Utah Saints! U-U-U-Utah Saints! U-U-U-Utah Saints!
U-U-U-Utah Saints! U-U-U-Utah Saints! U-U-U-Utah Saints!
U-U-U-Utah Saints! U-U-U-Utah Saints! U-U-U-Utah Saints!
U-U-U-Utah Saints! U-U-U-Utah Saints! U-U-U-Utah Saints!
U-U-U-Utah Saints! U-U-U-Utah Saints! U-U-U-Utah Saints!
U-U-U-Utah Saints! U-U-U-Utah Saints! U-U-U-Utah Saints!
U-U-U-Utah Saints! U-U-U-Utah Saints! U-U-U-Utah Saints!
U-U-U-Utah Saints! U-U-U-Utah Saints! U-U-U-Utah Saints!
U-U-U-Utah Saints! U-U-U-Utah Saints!*

Best wishes,

Utah Saints

*third draft

Dear The Bardots,

Notwithstanding that canonised skulls cannot fit atop Cornettos or 99s, I'm "getting close to feeling" that this is an "Obscenity Thing" which could have the constabulary "dragging me down to the" station.

Forgive me if I "Miss Another" lyric contradicting your statement, but "until somebody stops it", you should be thoroughly "Ashamed".

You may well be "Feeling Juvenile", but to demand that I "bring you the head of the saint in a gelati cone" would be to succumb to your criminal passion. Hopefully "you know I won't bother" to entertain it. Is this what you want from me, The Bardots?

I'm damned if you can bend me, as I've got a bad feeling about this.

Yours, hoping that you "Don't Let Me Down",

D Philpott

Dear Mr Philpott,

Thank you for your letter with its many weird references to my lyrics and song titles. I believe this is the first fan letter I have received since that one from Susan Reeves from Hull in 1996.

I'm not going to lie: Susan's letter was a lot more exciting - with its update on her boyfriend's demise and news of her new piercings.

Your letter suggests to me that you take things way too literally.

In The Bardots' song Caterina - with which you seem to have become obsessed - when I sing "bring me the head of the saint in a gelati cone" I am not intending this as a directive to Derek Philpott.

No. It was written following a chance encounter - whilst loafing around Europe in the late 1980s - with the severed head of Saint Catherine in a church in Sienna.

If my poetic response to this grim tete-a-tete is addressed to anybody, then it's the Catholic diocese of Tuscany. Or maybe their Boss. But definitely not you...

I do worry, Derek (if I may), that your solipsistic approach to listening to music must have caused you all sorts of difficulties over the years. Did you interpret "come on baby light my fire" as an invitation to head over to Jim Morrison's house and get his woodburner going? Did you assume that it was you who was personally responsible for making Madonna feel shiny and new?

By the way, the beatific bonce I stumbled upon most certainly would have fitted into an ice cream cone. It was pretty shrivelled up and mini. And anyway, have you seen the size of some of the ice cream cones in Italy?

Before signing off, can I just say how disappointed I am that you didn't pick up on the song's glaring error? 'Gelati' is plural, not singular. The line makes no sense. I dropped a clangore grammaticale.

Still. I'm glad I didn't spot it at the time. "Bring me the head of the saint in a gelato cone" would have been a nightmare to sing and made an ass(onance) of you and me.

Or something.

Yours,

Simon Dunford

(The Bardots)

Dear The Bevis Frond,

We all have "These Dark Days". When I was young, my friend Jimmy Clarke and I found ourselves going "Nowhere Fast" on the North Circular in his Punto after the brake caliper went at a pedestrian crossing in Portobello.

Trying to keep one's spirits up when the lights are changing and one's car is *not* being "Driven Away" is a "Thankless Task" The ~~Butt-head Branch~~ The Bevis Frond. Just sitting there "Doing Nothing" with no living soul helping us in the leaving of London was no way to keep us "high in a ~~Flat~~ Fiat".

There was no danger of a "Flood Warning" though; the engine hadn't stalled and the exhaust was blowin' smoke... thus negating your enquiry, "what keeps the motor running after the wheels have locked?".

Yours, now well out of it,

D Philpott

Dear Mr Philpott,

Thank you for your letter of 30.8.23. I was suitably impressed with canny inclusion of several of my song titles. May I start by saying that your tale about yourself and a certain Jim Clarke (not the former racing driver surely) having motoring problems on the North Circular seemed to me to be a work of pure fiction. The tell-tale clue was that when your brake caliper allegedly 'went', it could not have happened where you said it did. Portobello is in Edinburgh and The North Circular is in London, so this is clearly untrue. If, as I suspect you will say, you were referring to Portobello Road in West London, it is still inaccurate, as the North Circular, at no point crosses the aforementioned market street.

I am also somewhat dismayed by the fact that you would see fit to include a Beavis & Butthead reference. This is a frequent misconception, which appears to base itself on the fact that the names of my band and that of the American cartoon series are similar. A 'Bevis' is a variety of fern, and has nothing whatsoever to do with the Transatlantic so-called comedy programme. Also, 'Bevis' rhymes with the Scottish mountain Ben Nevis, while 'Beavis' (of Butthead notoriety) rhymes with Glastonbury Farm's Michael Eavis.

Having said all this, I admired the way in which you connected your Punto with 'High In A Fiat'. Very amusing.

But alas, I cannot see how the lack of a 'flood warning' (a somewhat tenuous link I feel) coupled with your non-existent car having an engine with an exhaust malfunction negates my philosophical question of what occurs after 'the wheels have locked'.

In fact, I find it rather presumptuous that you would think that this particular question was actually directed at you (someone I have never met and have no wish to) and your bogus vehicle.

May I just conclude by stating that although much of your unwarranted missive was nothing short of impertinent, I did actually enjoy its youthful foolishness, and appreciate that you actually thought it was worth sending to me.

Yours respectfully,

Nick Saloman

(Mistakenly referred to in your letter as The Bevis Frond, which is, in fact, the name of the combo in which I play)

Dear The Nightingales,

I hope that you do not think me "Bang Out Of Order" in stating that the shape-shifting attributes with which you associate me are really "No Can Do".

As far as superpowers go, "It's A Cracker", but I guess I'm just a little overcome to have been credited with metamorphical talents exceeding even those of "Great British Exports" that have done very well in Las Vegas or at a lucrative "private party".

It brings me no "Comfort And Joy" at all to formally confirm that I am neither a locomotive lavatory, a Scandanavian law enforcement officer or a token trinket tradesman.

"Joking Apart", I therefore refute your allegations that I am a toilet in the train, the Swedish Police and a souvenir seller.

Yours, hoping not to leave you "Down In The Dumps",

D Philpott

Dear D Philpott

Fancy hearing from you after all this time. I have my suspicions that you're still the same old crook, trying to rinse unpopular bands like ourselves of what you can... even forcing us to reply to your bizarre letters. The only reason I am even entertaining this is because you'll print the band's name in a book... I am shameless after all.

It brings me great joy to burst your bubble and tell you that these songs are not about you, Philpott... despite what those voices in your head are yelling. Please allow me to direct you to some of our other tracks that you may identify better with - *'Thicko Rides Again'* / *'You Don't Know What You're Doing'* / *'What A Carry On'*.

If you're trying to get something from us and think we've made some cash since 'King Rocker' you'd be wrong - we just 'Needed The Money At The Time' and, frankly, are still broke and still as unpopular in the grand scheme of things.

Don't quit the day job, 'Company Man'.

Fliss

Dear Thee Hypnotics,

I've listened to your Greek Amphitheatre percussion homage "All Night Long", or at the very least a total of nine times.

At the risk of being considered "All Messed Up" or that you will come down heavy upon me, I would like to "Choose My Own Way" to devise a Thing 4 U, as a "Testimonial" to "Phil's Drum Acropolis". Utilising ancient historical monuments "Unearthed" from "Coast To Coast" via Google Earth ~~Blues~~, I propose "Phil's Crash Cymbal (Revolution) Stone-henge", "Phil's Floor Tom Leaning Tower of Pisa", "Phil's Hi-Hat Hanging Gardens of Babylon" or, controversially, "Phil's Click Track Taj Mahal", as "What To Do" for a potential concept 7" single.

Please "Don't Let It Get You Down" if my "Preachin' & Ramblin'" syncopation structures are insufficient to "Tie It Up"; I can apply "The Big Fix" if required.

Yours mesmerisingly,

D Philpott

Dear Mr Philpott,

The history of the outfit can be summed up in a few words. For two Catholic boys who both narrowly avoided getting bummed at reform school, the lads done good to leave

Sunday school and form a musical ensemble. They ended up in a Red Hot Chilli Peppers song due to their look. It didn't stop there. They all wore black nylon socks and carried round sweaty cheese sandwiches wrapped in cling film. Jim once got voted as the singer with the best conditioned hair and Will and Ray got mistaken for book ends. They looked more like Afghan Hounds. The drummer Phil had two names; Phil... and the other being Malcolm Stotts or Stottsie for short. It stuck. Jim would often bark, "Leave it Stottsie you cunt, we don't want any trouble" when Malcolm had one of his volatile episodes. Will, who had a girlfriend, eventually became Cliff. Clear Headed Cliff to be precise. He always knew what to order for breakfast and had a year's supply of Marmite in his kitchen cupboard. This drove the rest of the band crazy. All Ray kept in his cupboard was cat food. The lads suggested Ray change his name to Roger - classic British, but he wouldn't have it. Then came the 'Let's Change The Name Of The Band' period. They became The Wycombe Stallions for a short spell. Then one night at CBGB'S they became The Kent Dorfman Legacy. Jim adopted the habit of dousing Phil in cold water on stage. This proved handy when, one night in France, Phil caught fire while playing the fans' favourite Justice In Freedom. As time wore on, Will decided that he, like Pete Townsend, wanted to smash his bass up. He did so, but would end up playing a small scale Fender Jag bass copy which he eventually smashed up in Berlin. Earlier that same evening, Phil got bitten by a dog backstage. The band had an alter ego, Ted Franks and the Private Dicks, inspired by a spirited episode of Lance Link Secret Chimp they saw in Washington DC.

Thee Hypnotics

Dear ~~Halley's Profit~~ Comet Gain,

I have never spent "Another Weekend" as dreadful as that babysitting our neighbour's granddaughter Kylie (who's aged "Just Fourteen"), and another girl, Charlie, ~~Asteroid Addition~~ Comet Gain.

The "Music Upstairs" last night, aptly called "Grime", was "White Noise" that sounded like "Aliens At War", ~~Fireball Bonus~~ Comet Gain. In my defiance, "If I Had A Soul" compilation that was "Unbroken" I would with "Some Intent" have played some "Footstompers" that never die on my gramophone in retaliation.

She had a million and nine such abominations stored on her telephone (purchased not as a Comet Gain but at a Curry's Discount), so I cannot imagine a day "when she turns on her first record player"!

I hope that you "Get Yourself Together" sufficiently to respond "If Not Tomorrow" then certainly without a "Wait 'Til December".

Yours,

D Philpott

Dear Idiot,

You have the wrong bloody address - I don't know how many times I've had to reply to this s*** but I HAVE NO IDEA WHAT YOU'RE GOING ON ABOUT! I'm a simple bloke from East Finchley in North London and I wish you tossers would stop hassling me with these abstract, obtuse THINGS. Okay, I was once a member of the local Rosicrusian cult - we used to meet in the woods and allegedly kill a few deer and allegedly do weird stuff to hedghogs but only in the later stages of the Solstice whatever that actually is, and yes perhaps our bloodletting led to a temporal portal opening in the fabric between psychedelic dimensional ruptures of reality but what the f*** do you expect from the suburbs? Eh?! We're not all sex fiends you know - so I looked into this "Comet Gain" thing and they're even worse than what we do (I ain't mentioning the rabbits thing we do). What a bunch of pasty faced losers! I tried listening to their inept rubbish but it just made my bladder shrivel - I grew up on the delightful melody of The Carpenters and Peters and Lee and THIS my friend is drivel.. is this 'punk rock'? Whatever it is it's a disgusting dog poo of sound - I played it to my daughter and she drew a pentagram and then sha* on it – disGUSTing.

So delete my contact - if this is a scam you have the wrong person. I will hunt you down and be extremely aggressive at your front door for a few minutes.

I don't know ANYTHING about this awful 'Comet Gain' but if I did I would recommend a beating followed by correctional …stuff … just make sure they bloody STOP.

Yours sincerely,

ANONYM

Dear The Dentists,

There are a "Tremendous Many" diversions for kids, apart from dolls and Hungry Hippo, designed to "Calm You Down" and ensure that "The Fun Has Arrived".

By no means "A Strange Way To Go About Things", it's all coming down to children making "The Best Of Everything". This is perhaps "something that will never happen" for future generations glued to screen games and reading the news about celebrities on their mobile phones, oblivious to a second Big Bang or impending event to make the "Whole World Explode".

You took me by surprise therefore in stating that Mary won't come out to play because all her toys are locked away.

You can "Have It Your Own Way" but I used to love Hide and Seek on a beautiful day, with flowers around me, enjoying "Everything In The Garden".

Yours, dreading that you're "Not Coming Back",

D. Philpott

Dear D Philpott

Thank you for your rather confusing letter.

On the one hand, you are correct in saying that we encouraged the more pastoral and healthy delights of an outdoor lifestyle for our nation's youth.

On a Beautiful Day one can of course take advantage of nature's wonders, such as the Strawberries, Daffodils, Butterflies, Basil, Apples, Tangerines, Flowers (around you, me or anyone else) and indeed Everything in The...yes, you get the picture.

Oh, and of course chickens (you bastard).

However it is untrue and frankly a slur to imply that we would advocate the locking away of toys. Indeed, in that song we're clearly lamenting the unfortunate situation that Mary found herself in.

The fact that you have neglected to appreciate the importance and significance of the Meccano-styled Little Engineer's Set demonstrates that you are clearly a weirdo (at any speed).

Yours,

Bob Collins

The Dentists

Dear The Supernaturals,

Your yelled threat, "You'd Better Smile", seventeen times per chorus, is counter-productive in that "Negativity" and fear of reprisals is unlikely to elicit a joyous expression.

I sympathise on another matter. We go to Ringwood car boot sales on "Monday Mornings" and just bought some chess board tea towels. We found, "Well Well Well" after the first hot wash that "everything's gone grey but used to be so black and white".

Finally, my Fortean friends, on a beach stroll as part of what we did last summer, I thought it was "Curtains" for a pedalo cast astray by a freak wave. One doubts that the hapless sailors' private affairs were in a state of disarray, so your claim, "your life's a mess, you've been cut adrift", is unfounded.

Although "It Doesn't Matter Anymore" I look forward to your response.

Yours, beseeching, "Please Be Gentle With Me",

Derek Philpott

Dear Derek,

Thanks for your letter. I have to say that no one has ever misinterpreted our lyrics quite as spectacularly as you. This song, "Smile", took at least 3 minutes to write and after putting so much hard work into our art we feel insulted that you have written such a wrong headed letter to us.

It's interesting that you mention pedalos. These boats sum up what's bad about life. You pedal furiously for days on end and find yourself back where you started. You think the ride on one will be fantastic when it is actually the most mundane seaborne experience you could ever have. Finally you get into a sweat over the fact that you'll have to pay the attendant an extra 50p for having overrun your short ride. In fact, your letter feels like a ride on a pedalo.

It's also curious that you mention we repeat "Smile" 17 times in the chorus of that song. Our music was never complicated enough to have a prime number lurking in there somewhere, although where I'm not sure. The band member who could officially count, our drummer Alan, told us it was actually 24 times and we took his word for it at the time. Interestingly enough our producer emphasised that we had to drill the word relentlessly into the public consciousness and that "even a pensioner with their hearing aid turned off" should be able to understand it.

I'm glad you mentioned that Car Boot Sale in Ringwood. We sold all our knackered old equipment there 15 years ago to a Christian Rock band with a very attractive female singer. Was that your daughter?

Anyway, please dont write to us again as we're busy.

The Supernaturals

Dear New Fast Automatic Daffodils,

In 'Jaws', when the shark devours its victims alive (as the fish's eyes roll up), this does not "create a mild sensation" or just "Aches and Pains". The hapless prey, internally screaming, "What Kind of Hell Is This?", didn't need reminding that they were being consumed whilst fully conscious.

I'm trying to kill my instincts, but am incredulous that you should warn a packed Hacienda crowd to watch out for the lions because they are being fed to the lions in 1990.

Also, assuming that these foolish things are bobbing up and down in agony, we cannot after a "Left Right" pan on the YouTube video, see any predatory hunters (we don't mean Tony Wilson) or wild animals (other than perhaps Messrs Ryder and their cohorts).

On an unrelated note to unseen carnivorous beasts, in order to "Get Better" reactions from anti-GM types and prove that you're nice people to do business with, a name change to "Traditional Gradual Organic Daffodils" could set you out as men with qualities.

We trust that you will address this missive "Head On" and not chuck it away, just chuck it away.

Yours,

D Philpott

Dear Derek,

The truth will out. We had assumed that our shameful blood-soaked past was a secret that would follow us to the grave along with the vast unrecouped sum owed to our record company.

It all began one morning in Hulme when a mysterious parcel was stuffed through the letterbox of our drummer Pez's flat.

This bit is true incidentally. Wrapped in several sheets of damp newsprint was the less than fresh remains of a herring. The words 'Beware the devil's fish claw' and 'Fishes eyes will watch your lies' were scrawled on the newspaper.

A lesser band might have dismissed this as the work of one of the many nutcases who lived thereabouts but we took it as something more serious; an invitation from the Devil himself. Pez was duly sent off to the nearest set of crossroads in the hope that a meeting with Satan might result in a deal that would ensure the success of the band. We were to be disappointed.

Met instead by a spirit in the form of a giant, fiendish

chicken, he duly signed away his soul and (rather carelessly we thought) the souls of the rest of the band.

In return he was given the promise of a two week number one slot in the Belgian radio charts at some unspecified time in the future, the assurance of 'a right good laugh' and the ability to play the drums very quickly while looking as though his head was about to drop off.

Our history as a band was littered with poor decisions; this was merely the worst.

We had indeed been nice people to do business with up until that point but so enraged were the rest of us at his callow foolishness that, the scales having fallen from our eyes, we resolved to abandon the meek Christian path that we had thus far followed and threw ourselves into an orgy of animalistic blood worship that only ended with the breakup of the band in 1995.

The chickens sacrificed to the depravity of our rhythm section; their number will never be known.

The 'alterations' perpetrated on French goats; the very mind recoils.

Until I received your letter I had thought to have buried and forgotten those other scenes of horror to which you allude. Reawakened from the depths of my unconscious mind, they crowd upon me and I fear for my sanity!

By way of compensating, we flirted outwardly with vegetarianism and remarkably little else. The prospect of a two week slot at number one in the Belgian radio charts is after all not a thing to be taken lightly and ultimately the Chicken God delivered; a fact that we are enormously proud of to this day. In addition, a video of ours was aired at least twice on late night European satellite TV and all it cost us was our eternal souls and around twelve grand. Our tour manager Mikey was tasked with making sure that everybody liked us, pointing out to Frenchmen that fish weren't vegetables and generally keeping things sweet.

The decision to actually start feeding our audiences to lions was with the benefit of hindsight, rather an own goal. It was 1992, the promised number one slot in the Belgian radio charts had not yet materialised and we felt that something drastic needed to be done; an act of faith that the Chicken God would be unable to ignore.

You'll be familiar with the scene in King Kong (also referenced in our hit single 'Music is Shit' and surprisingly not picked up on by yourself) where Fay Wray is tied to the sacrificial altar to lure Kong to his capture.

We played just such a trick on the Chicken God at our end of tour Hacienda gig, chaining a scantily clad Pez to his drum kit and making an even more bloody enormous horrible racket than usual in order to summon our tormentor and force him to deliver in his promise. It's on YouTube, though the footage ends just before the Chicken God appears and the fans are devoured by ravenous cats.

While successful in the short term, feeding your audience to wild beasts is no way to build a fan base and things could only go downhill from there on.

I think I should leave it there Derek. These are painful memories but there comes a time when one must unburden one's self and I feel as though a weight has been lifted, for which I can only thank you.

Yours nonsensically,

Andy Spearpoint,
New Fast Automatic Daffodils

Dear The ~~Anne Diamonds~~ Jack Rubies,

My nephew Dorian, a "Foolish Boy", sent me a photo of one of Oasis on a "Fascinatin' Vacation". I hope I never see the day that I find myself "Falling" for idiocy. He was "Lost In The Crowd" at Dealey Plaza, covered in green turf, and captioned "Grassy Noel".

This led me to google JFK and then your good selves. Unless it's gone "Over My Head", there have been no survivors of the Tudor treason triple threat torture package. Your claim therefore that to be hung, drawn, and quartered would be a fate that you would endure to be with me is surely "The Folly, The Folly!" of the harshest order.

You then describe the barbaric execution option as merely "uncomfortable and awkward". This is akin to Marie Antoinette, although she took grave exception, whining of a post-guillotining slight itch in 1793.

I'm sorry that you "got so confused" and sincerely hope that you will not disregard this as a "Crazy Letter" or retreat to your Hidey-Hole.

Yours, acting alone,

D. Philpott

Dear Phil & Dorian,

Hello there, and apologies for the capital punishment confusion.

Sadly, there is some rather blatant and downright reckless artistic license employed in the lyrics that you have referenced.

We would refer you to the second verse:

"To be drowned in murky water would of course make my life shorter, but I would gladly sink below to be with you", which, although also factually a fib, does at least infer the protagonist's demise is by their own hand rather than at the whim of a gaggle of medieval bully boys.

Speaking of Noel Edmonds and his "multi-coloured" grassy lawn, this seems a bit blurry.

We preferred Tiswas as our Saturday morning conspiracy romp, and have always maintained that Spit the "dog" was innocent.

We have all been card carrying members of the Sally James fan club since the previous century.

Many a bitter and twisted night, as we shivered, teeth chattering, huddled together for warmth in our Hidey Hole, we cheered ourselves with theatrical retellings of the Phantom "Flan" Flinger sagas.

I hope this clears things up. Please don't attempt any of the idiotic remedies for unrequited love we may have suggested in the past.

Seasons Greetings,

Sapphire & Steel

Dec 13, 2022

The Jack Rubies
℅ Dealey Plaza Club
13 Hobbs End
Lepers Leap,
N. Wales
C86 9XX

Dear ~~Particular Pollutant!~~ This Poison!,

There's a "Question Mark" over your lyrics, ~~Relevant Ricin!~~ This Poison!. "I'm Not Asking" for written transcripts, so have been "Poised Over The Pause Button" on YouTube.

Apart from Tom the cartoon cat when suffering "the fierce crack" over his head from his rodent nemesis Jerry, ~~Talked About Toxin!~~ This Poison!, felines do not emit tears of sadness, despite what "You Think".

Despite some search "engine failure", I have heard you state that "everyone will cry except for the cat", ~~Scrutinised Scourge!~~ This Poison!.

Yours hoping "It'll All Work Out",

D Philpott

Dear Mr Pott, or can I call you Phil?,

Thank you for your letter which arrived at This Poison! HQ this morning.

The lyrics to our songs are a closely guarded secret and an internet search (no matter which engine you use) is quite, quite, futile.

You cannot simply search on line for these works of lyrical genius penned by a wordsmith only (just) bettered by Oscar Wilde... our Saigz!! (Side note: Saigz now lives in a cave in the Apalachian mountains counting his blessings using his fingers).

Mystical, Powerful, Other-Worldly: words quite often rarely used to describe This Poison! lyrics.

They can and should only be read, uttered, sung by the writer himself. For it is he, our Saigz, and he alone that can bring those words to life, give them depth, make them sing, soar and shout to the rooftops.

As a wise man once said:

"He who disagrees with me in private, call him a fool. He who disagrees with me in public, call him an ambulance."(Simon Munnery)

En conclusion (that's French for in conclusion):

Let those with ears use them. Let them interpret, decipher, contemplate, mis-hear the poetry of This Poison! And decide for themselves. For it is them, the people, who should judge for themselves the majestic might, gargantuan depth and massive attack!!

Until we meet again and the case is SOL-VED.

Take it easy Phil. Speak soon.

This Poison!

Dear The Bodines,

I recently spent "hour after hour by the phone in the window" of my Citroen listening to "Tall Stories". In the end I was convinced I'd "Heard It All".

Without "Naming Names", at first we were friends when I reported a slip sliding clutch; then we were enemies. When "What You Want" is an idea of when the recovery vehicle is arriving on the A57 at Glossop, it does feel like you're being "Played" if you wait so long that it seems like "the seasons come and go".

In answer to your enquiry, therefore, "How then can hell be compared to limbo?", I would posit that you have never been a member of "Britain's fourth emergency service"!

Yours, God Bless,

Derek Philpott

Dear Mr Philpott,

As we made very clear in our legendary C86 song 'Therese', when stuck on t'Snake Pass, you must "keep cool when confusion mounts".

If "I've come to understand you" correctly, you seem to be confusing "weeks for days" and perhaps minutes for seconds, which "seems to count towards your confusion"...

In short, "You really must learn to curb your trust".

Although it sounds like the clutch pedal is "shaking, rattling and everything" and the "balance sways, the weeks are days", this really is no cause to "scare the health out of you...". In terms of cost, "although too much it never amounts" to more than a few hundred quid. Unless you are towed to Dodgy Dave's garage, but least said... "it's a touchy issue, you're pulling on scar tissue".

Yours,

Paul Brotherton, The Bodines

Dear Adorable,

My neighbour Janice Summers was pulled over on a bitterly cold night after a Christmas work's outing, for a faulty nearside rear bulb.

WPC Simmons asked, "Have You Seen The Light?", and Janice attempted a cool front, but "Everything's Fine, it's not a crash site" were the words to come stumbling out of her frozen mouth. She had to prove that she hadn't been drinking. After pleading with Simmons to "Go Easy On Her" and slurring that she should "Lettergo", Janice inhaled on the tube in a vain attempt to keep the meter in the blue and green.

That you "took a breath onto a canvas" also displays respiratory ignorance, although with my hand upon my heart, I do not have a vendetta to cut up your words with my butter knife. Even if I did, I don't think you'd care less!

Obsessively Yours, writing from home, boy,

D. Philpott

Dear Mr Philpott,

Thank you for your recent correspondence with regards to your friend Janice's altercation with an officer of the law.

Piotr did intend to write back in person via the postal service, but alas too many of his letters don't get sent, and consequently there are too many letters that don't get read, which leads to a surfeit of letters under his bed, that quite frankly make it hellishly difficult to clean his room, and so he has asked me to reply to you via email on his behalf.

He noted the coincidence that so many of the events seemed to tally with either titles or lines from Adorable songs, which seemed quite remarkable, or possibly willfully contrived in order to illicit a response, and he also asked to pass on his regards to Janice, whilst reminding her to keep her car in roadworthy condition.

Just as a side note, you'll find that the line is "*I drew* a breath onto a canvas" not "*I took* a breath onto a canvas...", which makes better sense (in a dreamy poetic arty-farty aren't-I-good-at-punning? sort of way). Spec Savers have free hearing tests, which you can do online and may help avoid similar problems in the future.

Yours sincerely

Jeff Henderson-Smythe

(PA to Mr Piotr Fijalkowski of Adorable)

Dear Mr. Hindmarsh,

I concede that "endless possibilities" normally exist, but there's lots of information online about the doomed German dirigible's "Last Day On Earth".

There were some shoddy Zeppelins but this was one of the "Good Ships", steered sensibly (not by a "swervedriver"), and the official documentation is easily sourced. "You Find It Everywhere" on the internet that the explosion, resulting allegedly from faulty wiring, or if you will, a "Badearth", did not occur in "These Times", but on the 6th of May 1937.

It may therefore "Feel So Real" to you Sir, but unless your account is attributable to an apparition or perhaps your "99th Dream", it is quite impossible that "somewhere up in the sky The Hindenburg still flies".

Yours, hoping not for a "Single Finger Salute",

Derek Philpott

Sir,

Respectfully, you are talking hot air.

I have suspected this matter to be *Bubbling Up* within you for some weeks, but consider your argument simply for *The Birds*.

Many years ago, *In My Time* with Swervedriver, we met a most excellent fortune teller - he arrived unannounced at one of our concerts with a *Girl, on a Motorbike*. *Harry & Maggie* were their names, I seem to remember.

It was Harry who informed us that the Hindenburg had, in fact, risen again, apparently piloted by none other than Elvis Presley (aka *The Other Jesus*). It was such a thrilling moment. We were so adrenalised. *You Never Lose That*

Feeling, you know.

It is on Harry's advice that we had relied when making said assertion. If, however, it transpires that this advice is found to be apocryphal, then can I ask that you contact Harry (details attached), challenge him to a *Duel* and, should you prevail, *Bring Me The Head of The Fortune Teller?* Misinformation, as we all know, has always been around. *You Find it Everywhere*, in fact. That, however, does not ever make it excusable.

As you know, Sir, I am no longer engaged with said indie beat combo. These days I run a car dealership, specialising in Jaguars. E-Types mainly. Fords too. Mustangs, Capris and Zephyrs. *My Zephyr* is a particularly fine example of the model.

Enough of this frippery. I must get on. Can't do everything. Who do you think *I Am? Superman?*

Sincerely,

Jez Hindmarsh

Dear The ~~Broth Basilisks~~ Soup Dragons,

Please find attached a summons that I received from Salisbury Magistrates Court after foolishly heeding your "Mindless" motoring advice just a fortnight ago, The ~~Mulligatawny Mythical Creatures~~ Soup Dragons.

"Don't go the wrong way" helped when entering a "One Way Street", but I don't own "an automatic machine", ~~The Ham & Leak Hydras~~ Soup Dragons... so I did "keep on driving higher" in 5th gear and couldn't "Get Down Get Down" to less than 40mph, or touch the brakes "Softly", The ~~Vegetable Wyverns~~ Soup Dragons. I didn't see "15 colours in front of me" – just a "red light shine", ~~The Cream of Mushroom Komodos~~ Soup Dragons.

To "just take a chance and make it fast" has not left me free to do what I want any old time. I've had to resort to my wife's pushbike, as she "puts me through her cycle", The ~~Dill Dumpling Drakes~~ Soup Dragons.

Yours, soon unable to "keep moving every day",

D Philpott

Dear Mr Philpott,

Thank you for your note, which we have distributed across the *Whole Wide World*.

We feel however that many of the claims in your summons are deeply unfounded and we'd like to suggest the following course of action to redress the balance:

Firstly, given the state of the world's climate emergency, we are *Pleasantly Surprised* that you have switched to new gear and resorted to using your wife's pushbike. The simple facts are that if we continue to behave in our old ways there will be *No Music On A Dead Planet*, so we suggest that we treat *Mother Universe (Divine Thing)* with the deepest respect... and for this we fully commend your future actions.

We further recommend seeking out more *Pleasure*, but without taking *Another Dream Ticket*. This can instead be achieved by exploring your local cycle routes and perhaps doing a sponsored cycle raising some money for a good cause. If this is not possible we may have to take the action to ask you to Vacate My Space.

Love Is Love,

Sushil K Dade

(on behalf of The Soup Dragons)

Dear The Aardvarks,

I am not a qualified pilot, so your invitation, "You Can Fly My Plane", has to be the most irresponsible I have heard since Mr. J. Lennon appealed to an infant to helm his Rolls Royce.

Also, a flimsy dinghy is unlikely to withstand the rigours of interstellar travel, and oars within a vacuum would be ineffective. This leads me to "Hold On" to a disbelief that you ever "rowed around the Universe in a boat made for two".

Indeed, I'm "On My Way" to concluding that you are so "in the dark" about transportation that future "cover versions" could include "Up, Up And Away In My Beautiful Saloon", "Rock The Chopper (Don't Tip The Helicopter Over)" or "I've Got A Static Caravan, You Can Ride It If You Like".

Yours, hoping to hear "When The Morning Comes",

Derek Philpott

Dear Mr Philpott,

Firstly, I must thank you for drawing attention to the Varks' peculiar relationship with transportation. Years before singer (and writer) Gaz bought his first aeroplane, he developed an embarrassing obsession with flight. Being West Londoners, we'd bunk off school and head over to Heathrow Airport, where Gaz would sit for hours in his cagoule - hood up with flask of Bovril by his side - excitedly writing down aeroplane numbers. Meanwhile, the rest of the Varks used statically-charged bent spoons to electrically shock Pac-Man machines out of hundreds of free credits.

Shortly after Gaz bought the plane, his shameless showing off began; he'd invite young ladies to sit on his lap while taking them on a few low loops over the Thames Valley

Sewage Works. Thankfully the authorities made him attend an aviation-cum-woke rehabilitation course before too much harm was done.

Regarding those mysterious excursions with Arthur C Clarke...well...a little known secret for you Derek: the oars were just decoys! Arthur pre-loaded us with copious amounts of baked beans, laced with something which he sprinkled from a glass jar, hand-labeled "Top Secret: Human Propulsion Formula" - but underneath, an earlier label, only just visible, read "Dr Leghorn's Beefing Powders". Arthur had to keep pulling bassist, Jason, from one side of the boat to the other by his ears - curiously, this prevented the boat from going round in circles... all very strange.

Life is much quieter now Derek, but some things haven't changed: Gaz runs the Suburban Garden Twitchers Club - the birds really love his fat-balls (but they do hang very low and the local cats keep going for them too!).

Well, I do hope that helps clarify a few things for you Derek.

Yours,

A Vark

Dear Thousand Yard Stare,

I've got my "Hands On" your seminal soccer stalemate 7" single, "No Score After Extra Time". "I'll begin" by stating that I'm "nonplussed". The inflated proboscis/ triumph aroma episode is a cause for "Wonderment".

Even if a "Small Change", olfactory organ expansion due to odour is sure to confuse one and all. That an all-conquering cologne, winning whiff, or successful stench can administer defeat does, ~~Millennium Gawp~~, Thousand Yard Stare, "smell a bit off".

If however "your nose is swelling with the scent of victory" owing to a poisoned parfum, biohazardous CHANEL №5 or "Tragedy No. 6", please alert Trading Standards to the toxic Laboratoire, ~~Half-Mile Ogle~~ Thousand Yard Stare. It must get its "Come Uppance"!

I sincerely hope that the bloated protuberance can at least be reduced to "Halfsize".

Yours,

D. Philpott

Dear Mr Philpott,

<u>Re: Nose Matters</u>

Thank you for your kind letter. As you probably know, the trope of proboscitic enbiggenment has a long and historical precedent.

From the proto-Freudianism of the woodenly priapic Pinnochio, surely a response to his troubled father-son relationship (the oedipal pinnochio?) to the thematically connected considerations of the nose in Tristram Shandy - where the narrator teases the reader with whether the nose in question is a stand in for the phallus - to many others, there is a rich history of this idea.

Lear's 'Dong with the luminous nose' surely makes the psycho sexual component clearer, and in Cyrano de Bergerac we find a protagonist whose nose size inhibits his romantic life. In Gogol's 'The Nose' a man's nose detaches from his body and goes about an independent life.

But with the nose comes, as you note, the smell. Surely a derridean binary if ever there was one. Paradoxically the smell ceases to exist without the nose and the nose would not evolve without the need to detect the smell. Or in Deleuzean terms, we find that the smell and the nose territorialise and de-territorisalise each other forming a machinic assemblage, a 'Small Change' indeed. What then is the smell? And if the smell and the nose deterritorialise each other are we left with what Deleuze and Guitar call the 'body without organs', or a face without a nose? Is this a metaphor for the problem of intra species co-operation or is it a football match?

We hope this makes everything clear.

With love,

Thousand Yard Stare

Dear The Trudy,

It may soon "Dawn" on some suffering from "Tunnel Vision" that there are "Things To Do" so as to correct your crimson crew commander combustion claim.

"What I'm Going To Do Today" is simply state the "So Obvious". "Girls Who Fall Apart" may well refer to early Lady Penelope or Aqua Marina off of Stingray prototypes. Also, every story ever told regarding 'Captain Scarlet' - "All Grown Up & Broken Down" by multiple skirmishes with Mysteron "Bad Boys" - recounts the hapless puppet to be constructed from naturally fire-resistant fibreglass, thus negating your statement that "his body may burn".

Furthermore, in order to get her "What She Wants" for Christmas in 1975, my friend Tony Beasley bought his daughter the mail order figurine from up town and lost its head even before he got back to ~~Action Stations~~ Acton Station - a dirt cheap malady that was anything but "In-des-tructible"!

Yours,

D Philpott

Dear D. Philpott,

I'm afraid that I had to shred The Trudy's reply to your letter, as some of it was indecipherable and the parts I could make out were rubbish.

Unbelievably, their attempt at a reply suggested that I am a Machiavellian character who had brainwashed them into thinking they were from outer space by relentlessly making them watch Blake's 7, Doctor Who, Lost in Space and every Gerry Anderson series. Apparently, that's how they came to love the Captain Scarlet theme tune, which they released as a single in the 80s.

The Trudy said that a few years later they suddenly remembered that they aren't from another planet after all. They reckon they painted themselves into a sci-fi corner back then and it's nice to be able to write about other subjects nowadays, like nature and feelings, or some-such. Worst of all was their assertion to be making music just for the joy of creating something that they really believe in, and about how proud they are of a newish song called 'Dear Sancho'. Their letter was ridiculous, so I'm replying myself.

I was concerned that the apparent contradiction you mentioned in the Captain Scarlet lyrics opened The Trudy up to a class-action lawsuit under The Trade Descriptions Act, by the 33⅓ people* who bought the record. However, they didn't write it: the late, great Barry Gray, who composed the music for most Gerry Anderson shows, did. Barry was a genius, and let's face it, no-one would seriously criticise him for fear of incurring the displeasure of International Rescue, Spectrum, SHADO, WIN, WASP, and other powerful organisations too numerous to mention.

Regarding your friend Tony Beasley; even though the Captain Scarlet figurine fell apart, he was very enlightened in buying a male action figure for his daughter in the 70s.

Narrow-minded gender stereotyping of the time would have led most parents to buy their daughters something based around the female aeronauts from the series.

Bearing that in mind, I have every 'Symphony' for your friend's plight, as his little 'Angel' deserved better. To restore 'Harmony,' I have enclosed a 50p record token and I would be grateful if you would travel back to 1975 and 'Interceptor', sorry, intercept him, so that he can buy a copy of Bohemian 'Rhapsody' for his daughter instead. This is an excellent 'Melody', and the record will definitely not destruct before he reaches his 'Destiny-ation'.

Love

Bexx Bissell, Self-Appointed Manager to The Trudy

*I couldn't figure it out either but that was the official sales figure for the singles chart.

Dear ~~Mr. Schmidt Messerschmitt~~ Spitfire,

I had "Minimal Love" for my Steve Austin toy as a kid; I preferred my battery-powered Evel Knievel. Being a Christmas gift, it was literally a "Free Machine". I never saw adverts for a "Rubber Rosie".

Little Lee Majors was a "Bare Doll", spending "some days with nakedness" because I'd dress my Action Man in his orange tracksuit. My dad once told me, "Hey Go Easy" when I dropped him on the patio, knocking out his "Translucent" bionic eye, ~~Spotfear~~ Spitfire.

I was nevertheless very impressed with your 'cover version' of the programme's theme tune, although to allow for inflation since 1975 this would ideally need to be rerecorded as the "34,091,933 Dollar Man".

Yours, hoping not to have hit a "Dead End",

D. Philpott

Dear D. Philpott,

That's quite the fixation on hyper-macho toys from the 1970s you have. But I suppose you have every right to think that I might have the same obsession. After all, Spitfire had a reputation for hard living and hard loving.

Admittedly, wearing the tightest leather trousers in town and taking two go-go dancers on a tour of the toilet circuit probably didn't help. Yet nothing could have been further from the truth.

In reality, my brother Nick (bass) and I were brought up in a gender-neutral, inclusive environment; our parents were early advocates of gentle parenting and natural consequences. We were a far cry from being typical boys; Nick's favourite childhood toy was a Girls' World hair styling head and I liked nothing more than to curl up with Radio 3 and the London Review of Books.

Sadly, the band was little more than a product of the capitalist music industry. Our original proposal to the label was that our debut single be a cover of the 'Bionic Woman Theme' arranged for string quartet and woodwind. Unfortunately, our hand was forced, and we ended up with the tone perfect, corporate garage-punk version of the 'Six Million Dollar Man' you so admire.

To be honest, I was disappointed at the cultural desert that was the 90s rock and roll scene. I suppose demands are demands and silk sheets don't buy themselves.

Also, strictly between you and I, when we were booked for our first Peel session, John phoned before the recording with a very insistent song request. Forget The Undertones or the Fall; even in 1991 he was still Rod Stewart obsessed. "No 'Legs', no session" - his actual words. So we abandoned plans to debut our visionary take on excerpts from Benjamin Britten's 'Peter Grimes', and, reluctantly, wheeled out a solid mercury version of 'Hot Legs'.

The folly of youth.

Yours etc.,

JP

Dear ~~Swinesiblings~~ ~~Hamhombros~~ Pigbros,

I'm "Not A Lot" impressed by "Skin Deep Theories" and didn't see things quite the same, ~~Rasherrelatives~~ Pigbros. I'm "Past Caring" about your virtuous viral vicar vitriol. That's "The Way Things Currently Are".

Apologies if this is a "Dumb Question" spawned by a "Bad Attitude" ~~Swillerstock~~ Pigbros, but I am "In Doubt". How may anyone meet an ill preacher from whom they may catch a religious fever?

Yours, looking to "put the world to right",

D Philpott

Dear Derek,

It was lovely to hear from you and well done for creating your letter entirely out of Pigbros song titles. OK, conceded, it didn't make a lot of sense but I do admire the effort!

Of course the English language is always evolving; you know, like that clever way of adding a number in a word to save all the trouble of spelling it correctly - which I think is gr8! Perhaps you've seen a future where, one day, we could all be communicating exclusively via the use of Pigbros titles? OK, we may have to somewhat restrict the subjects of our conversations - and I can now see the error of not writing more tunes called 'Are you going down the shop to buy a paper and a bottle of milk, oh and whilst you're there can you get me a Twix?'. That would have really helped with the whole communicating thing.

Mind you, you'd have no trouble if you required the purchase of 'Excessive amounts of alcohol'?! - Now, can you see what you've started?!

Nic, once of Pigbros

Dear Helen Love,

"Staying In" during the so hot "Golden Summer" of 2020 was hardly the "Happiest Time Of The Year", Ms. Love. Lockdown in my seaside town, even with my transistor radio on and windows open to "Let The Sunshine In", achieved only "A Quite Good Time".

I'm not "On My Own" in understanding your desire to go rollercoasting in the summertime when the weather's fine, but it's a "Red Light". Even if you "Jump Up And Down" to help circulation, "jeans hiked real high" or "Double Denim" are unsuitable attire in Swansea, and "sun cream from Tesco" is unnecessary.

"I Don't Want To Fight", Ms. Love, but urge you, lest you end up "black and blue", to stay ahead of the race and "Fly To New York", or another warmer "space girl".

Yours, hoping not to be told, "Shut Your Mouth",

D Philpott

Dear D. Phillpott,

Thanks for your recent letter. I assume you've taken a day off from writing to The Daily Mail.

I have to tell you that I have no intention of moving to warmer climes; the weather here in Swansea can be quite lovely in the Summer and a T-shirt can be worn without fear of catching a chill.

I have to say I was taken aback by your comment about Tesco Sun Cream being unnecessary. I can only think you must be one of those GB News, Lawrence Fox red-faced Donald Trump types that I have to continually block on twitter.

Can I maybe offer you a word of advice? The next time you venture outside in the Summer without a cardigan, apply a liberal amount of lotion to your exposed extremities and start taking the risk of skin cancer seriously.

Also, if having trouble locating sunscreen in Tesco, you'll find it on the same aisle as the incontinence pants you buy.

I do hope my advice helps you to stay *Ahead Of The Race* and you live a long, healthy, and generally unhappy life.

Helen.

Dear Hurrah!

<u>Re: White Collar Wastage</u>

I would if I could enjoy a "Better Time" waking up to the smell of fresh cut grass, a "Walk In The Park" and not having to suffer and see how many rivers "Around and Around" the planet are being polluted.

However, now the climate changes for the worse. It seems, "Sad But True", that "That Dream's Over Now".

Who'd have thought therefore that Jackie, who's a banker, and Jane, who's a clerk, would be sitting right down by the fire when they both get home from work, sending fossil fuel poisons into the "Big Sky"?

That "The Sun Shines Here", and the eco-unfriendly pair can buy solar panelling and "Get It On" the roof, makes me want to rub my face in the ground.

What I need, ~~Whoopee!~~ Hurrah!, for the sake of my "Sweet Sanity", is for you to bring the curtain down on this toxic twosome once and for all!

Do "Tell Me About Your Problems", with my address clearly marked, or to the sender they will return.

Yours,

D. Philpott

Sir,

While it's true that climate change is a pressing problem, I can assure readers that we did everything we possibly could to reduce any environmental impact.

We changed from coal powered guitar amplifiers to sustainably sourced peat.

We switched from metal guitar strings to ones wound from pubic hair, harvested from floors of public toilets (though I think it did contribute to us sounding out of tune for a lot of the time).

Instead of a gas guzzling tour bus we travelled by bicycle, although we were often several days late for a gig.

All our stage clothes were recycled and previously worn by The Grumbleweeds and The Rubettes.

But probably our greatest contribution to the saviour of the planet was that we recycled and reused music and lyrics.

Our credentials are there for all to see; even Sir David Attenborough said that Hurrah! were a group that had zero impact!

I rest my case.

Paul Handyside

Dear The Wake,

I must "Make It Loud" and "Talk About The Past" concerning your trims. It's a "Testament" to my sleuthing that I could "Sail Through" promotional photographs "looking for the trace" of a mohican or lacquered spikes – or their failed generation – but find that you all used to have very tidy short back and sides. In terms of colour they were in "Harmony" with mine before I turned old and grey.

I therefore severely doubt that you "fell from a stool in a pub where they played punk rock onto a floor that always flattens your hair".

I fear that your tale is not quite right, it is just an outrageous lie, and I hang my head in shame if found to be incorrect.

Yours abruptly, as I just heard "Something Outside",

D Philpott

Dear Mr Philpott,

Thanks for your forthright comments about The Wake's hairdos. By the way, congratulations on your research skills... it isn't easy to find promotional photographs of the group as we rarely publicise ourselves unless poked at with a stick, or, in this case, your letter.

We did indeed favour neat short-back-and-sides haircuts. The A&R departments and stylists at Factory and Sarah Records forced us to look sensible, trustworthy and prepared to undertake office work at any time. Eventually, our keyboard player Carolyn rebelled, growing her lovely hair long and leaving the rest of us in the fashion shade. Nevertheless, the boys never resorted to outrageous coiffures for attention, although I admit we experimented with wigs behind the scenes. As far as we're aware, all backstage photographs of that nature have been shredded. I trust, therefore, your missive is not a prelude to further blackmail communications? If so, I wish you all the best for the future, and hope your own mane can be restored to its original colour with the advancements of science.

Take care of your hair.

Caesar (for The Wake)

Dear ~~The Rural Rodents~~ Field Mice,

It's been "Snowball"ing and "my life was always heading for this" thanks to email, but I am so sorry that you're the last one to send the last letter ever.

Unless "You're Kidding Aren't You" The ~~Pasture Pests~~ Field Mice, I "Couldn't Feel Safer" in stating this to be a "Landmark" moment. I have no choice but to feel sorry for the delivery people that the Post Office will be "Letting Go" of for keeps at the "End Of The Affair". As "Bleak" as it is though, The ~~Countryside Critters~~ Field Mice, they won't reach "Freezing Point", starting work at five to six (that's what the time is) in the Winter when September is so far away.

Yours, much "Clearer", The ~~Vineyard Voles~~ Field Mice,

D. Philpott

Dear Mr Philpott,

Have you seen the price of a first class stamp recently? Indeed, it is a very sad and sorry state that some of the wonderful national institutions in this country are now serving private fat cats, and all at our expense.

Back to your letter; your references pre-date privatisation by at least a decade. Most of them, are indeed, quite "Bleak".

May I suggest, if you are feeling sad listening to the works of The Field Mice, that you move on through Bobby Wratten's discography to his most recent fayre, "Overwintering", which brings true wisdom and an acceptance of the world to bear.

And perhaps sit in a wood; you will find that they are very healing places.

Incidentally, The Wizard of Oz, Chapter 9, is entitled 'The Queen of The Field Mice'. If only her face could have been on a stamp. I'm sure it would have been a valuable collector's item.

I hope this may ease your worry of the world at large.

Yours Sincerely,

Anne Mari

Dear Red Lorry Yellow Lorry,

I've just shelled out £20 for a pair of Used 150 Watt Celestions which I hooked up to my Hi-Fi. I did "Feel A Piece" snap off, but, thinking there was "Nothing Wrong", couldn't resist the "Temptation" to turn on the mains, thinking it was all "Safe As Houses".

The turntable *was* "Spinning Round", but the speakers began to "crackle and burn" and I did "see the fire".

I thank you, "Hand On Heart" Red Lorry Yellow Lorry, for proving that I've been short-changed, there's only me to blame and "You Only Get What You Pay For".

Yours, "Cut Down",

D Philpott

Dear Derek,

Receiving your letter reminded me of a recent incident which involved a complete stranger coming up to me in a darkened room at a party.

There is something reassuring about bearing one's soul to a complete stranger… they don't carry the baggage our more enduring friendships carry.

"So which one are you, red bastard or yellow custard?" he asked.

I was slightly nonplussed by his impertinence; he was after all a total stranger. "You know what?" I said… "We are the MC5 Goes To Hollywood to meet Van Halen".

"So what really changed your life?", he asked. "Was it passing your 11 plus?"

"No way…" I replied "…it was seeing Jimi Hendrix perform at Woodstock, which inspired me and countless others like me to want to make a noise".

For us mere mortals who love noise, sound and posh hi-fi... We can only imagine how he must've felt that day with the Star-Spangled Banner coming out of his hands... but we had to try nonetheless.

Yours

David Wolfenden

Dear Shop Assistants,

My PC just died, so "it's the end" for a decade's worth of documents, I thought. Then, I remembered, "Lucky you've got a safety net" – external storage – so "clouds all cover the past ten years".

It therefore "seems I have to say" thank you for your 1985 prescience.

Yours, "with no hard(drive) feelings",

D Philpott

Dear Mr Philpott,

I'm sure you know the Shop Assistants existed in the 1980s and are literally the only band in the world never to reform.

We are sorry to hear about your dead policeman and hope you find a soulmate in the "Search Bar" which we assume is some kind of singles' club.

Love,

Shop Assistants

Dear ~~Juvenilejogger~~ Boyracer,

I'm "unable to speak" of a "Secret Joke", but feel "Short Changed", ~~Adolescentathlete~~ Boyracer. With every word uncovered, you've titled "Matty's Untitled Song". Its lack of a title is thus a "False Economy".

Furthermore, I "Don't Want No Trouble", ~~Minormarathonman~~ Boyracer, but your claim, "I Was The Drummer In Altered Images", proves you "careless and caught out", for that was Tich Anderson.

"Stand By Your Words", ~~Striplingsprinter~~ Boyracer. I don't "Ask Too Much" and this is not "Hatemail".

Yours, aware that "This Has Gone On Too Long",

Derek Philpott

Dear Mr Philpott,

Thanks for your interest. But I must stress I do "Stand By My Words", you cheeky scamp!

Growing up in a small Yorkshire town, surrounded by leafy green, sneaking cans of Skol from Dad's fridge and classic youthful boredom, my mind was primed to wander.

I did indeed spend my pre-teens daydreaming I was on Top of the Pops air drumming to Pinky Blue. My eyes were opened and the pop dream detonated inside my head.

(All the best bands are Scottish, as you know).

I duly honed my craft, albeit temporarily, until my life transformed after seeing the Marychain on The Old Grey Whistle Test, at the tender age of 14.

I promptly ditched my starchy classical guitar lessons, saved up my pocket money and bought a 49 quid guitar and a fuzzbox.

I was off and running.

I have spent the last 3 decades trawling the toilets of the world, celebrating my own hamfisted charm and confusing literally dozens of gorgeous people along the way.

So, in conclusion, you may be correct in assuming "This Has Gone On Too Long"...

But I guess I'm an indie lifer at this point.

Yours,

Stewart Boyracer

Dear ~~Pulled Pork~~ The Longpigs,

In the 70s I used to buy my wife Charlie. She went through 100s of grams of the stuff and went "On and On" if she couldn't get her hands on any, as a matter of fact. It was always a "cause for headaches" if she ran out, and she was not satisfied with herself or "Happy Again", until she had more to be sniffed.

Had your unnamed female used no cosmetics, her natural fragrance, exclusive to every individual, would "in essence" be her U.S.P. ("Unique Smelling Point"). You are correct - "there is no perfume she can buy to make her smell like herself".

However, "I don't like to be seen" as spouting "Blah Blah Blah", but that "she puts on perfume to smell like someone else" is, to use a "Dozen Wicked Words", ludicrous in that mass produced eau de toilette is worn by millions.

I must add "Loud and Clear" that you're not to wind yourselves up over an observation taken too "Far".

Yours,

D. Philpott

Sir,

You make a good point - in the 90s we used to rub Charlie all "Over Our Bodies" in an effort to appear more like "Gangsters", but just ended up smelling like someone else.

Since we found out that that "Wonder Drug" was "All Hype", we have settled into obscurity and taken up "Amateur Dramatics".

Perfumes in general never make scents (sic) to me: I can "Take It All" or leave it all, and as "Far" as I'm concerned they all merely combine some "Whiteness" with some "Sweetness" in an effort to fool one's palette.

Perhaps all we were ever looking for were "Blue Skies", and although I might have implied that I had nothing but contempt for journalists, in fact "I Lied - I Love You".

Ever Yours,

Simon Stafford

(Aged 47½)

Dear The Shop Window,

I have a loft full and nothing to play them on, and have done my best to "Disengage The Robots", but the facebook ads keep "calling out". I'm NOT looking for singles in my area, and it's "clear" that you, my reflective retail friends, are also considering your attic, as in "thinking of a space beyond the ceiling".

Mine too is "Out of Reach" (yeh) but does not suffer baffling perennial Arctic conditions. You state that "the ice won't melt" and "you'll feel the snow", so one hopes that a sodden skylight will not necessitate the need to "Break Down Walls" or "Evacuate".

Is there anywhere, The Shop Window, that I could put a postcard up to try and shift these 78s?

I look forward to learning the "Lay Of The Land".

Yours, ("I Realise") on display,

D Philpott

Dear Mr Feelpan,

Thank you for your letter; after about half an hour, and six read throughs of your ramblings, I finally gave in and asked my 6 year old if he could decipher it.

He said he thinks the silly man wants to clear out his loft!

We'll happily advertise your clearance of clutter via our 'shop window'.

It will be titled "Philpott's Lost Plot Over Loft 78s", with a bonus track on the flipside - 'Philpott's Been At The Pill Pot'.

We would hope to represent your confusing hodgepodge of garble with instruments that reflect it, such as Kazoo, spoons and a triangle, all overlaid with our signature Jangly guitars. This will surely help you clear a space above your ceiling as you desire, although we're feeling maybe you need to get outside more and not be in said loft alone. Sadly, we believe the ice will melt, so be sure to wear 'Philpott's Flip-Flops' when leaving your cave.

Hope this will help!

Best wishes,

Carl - The Shop Window

(Note: I'm not an actual shop window but one part of indie jangle-pop band 'The Shop Window')

Dear The Chesterfields,

<u>Full Structural Failure</u>

Sorry to put your "Nose Out Of Joint", but "When It All Comes Down" to it you appear to be a "Male Bimbo"!

I've got to hand it to you; if your "Bed Is An Island" in one of these "New Modern Homes" then even at "High Tide" a "Girl On A Boat" could still go "All The Way".

What's "Controversial" though is electrocution if exposed to "Slippery Track" wiring during a "Flood".

In fact, no part of your abode seems "safe to be seen"; sadly unsurprising from a "Pop Anarchy" combo whose brandname is "Besotted" with High Tar cigarettes!

Goodbye Goodbye for now!

D Philpott

Dear Derek,

How can you say that?

You've opened doors that should be closed.

I know your scheme; it starts with the ultimate devilish ploy - first a Facebook message and then a letter... but we will not be inviting you round to view our new modern home.

I'm not trying to hurt you dear, and I know you are in a class of your own when it comes to rejection, so we will allow a visit to the treehouse at the end of our garden.

It's waiting for you, detached and beautifully thatched, and with a quite pleasant view.

So wipe that sad expression from your face

Simon Chesterfield

The Chesterfields

Dear The Men They Couldn't Hang
Re: Walkin', Talkin'

Like all "Hardworking People", in terms of HMRC I aim to remain "Hard To Find" guilty and one of the men they couldn't harangue. I never "Fail To Comply".

I was about to invest my "10 Grand" savings "Overseas" in "A Place In The Sun" until "The Man In The Corner Shop" said to put it in my spouse's name. She can receive gross interest as a non taxpayer, and we would receive a small "Gold Rush".

You "don't wanna hear about my money or hear about my wife", but I need confirmation, The ~~Pierrepoint Dodgers~~ Men They Couldn't Hang. Your assertion, "there's nothing you can tell me that I don't already know" is untrue, so please "Come Forward".

I await with "Great Expectations" a reply tomorrow or "The Day After", my gallows exempt friends.

Yours, hoping you haven't got better things to do,

D. Philpott

Dear D. Philpott,

Thanks for your letter which I have read and reread a couple of times in an attempt to get to the nub of it all.

I think it's fair to say that none of The Men They Couldn't Hang are really in a position to provide any financial investment guidance to you at this time. However, when we were buskers, we firmly believed in the adage "look after the pennies and the pounds will look after themselves" and we would usually pop into the 'The Clarendon' or one of the other Hammersmith taverns and spend a penny or two on refreshments while planning our next move. If we were feeling particularly flush, we'd pop a handful of coins into the nickelodeon in the corner of the bar and maybe draw a little inspiration from that cherry red vinyl star jukebox.

However, if you happen to have a few quid burning a hole in your pocket, you couldn't go far wrong by joining us in a town near you and enjoying a show on our 40th anniversary tour. We will be giving plenty of advice from the stage based on everything learned over the past 4 decades - but almost certainly nothing of a commercial or fiscal nature. That said, we welcome you to make an investment at our well stocked merchandise stand and will be happy to accept cash or cards in exchange for goods that, we are certain, both you and your spouse will treasure for many years to come.

Thanks again for your letter.

Wishing you all the best,

Phil 'Swill' Odgers

The Men They Couldn't Hang

PS. To further illustrate how we don't give a damn about a greenback dollar we once turned down an offer of Roger Whittaker recording a version of 'Parted From You' - as I thought it would be a bad idea...

Dear The McTells,

Knowing my "Rotten" luck in not getting things the "Right Way Round", I'd just like to clarify whether "Virginia MC" is a rap singer or a powered bike.

You wish Virginia to "drive you down her Country lanes" and "over her village greens", presumably using "4th Gear Shift" after a "Jump Start". That implies the latter, although in the "Back Of My Mind" a cricket lawn "Smash Up" by heavy tyres on "such a lovely day" during nice "English Weather" is not on.

That you are conversing with her, and "she's so pretty", however, does go "Side By Side" with a human subject, and perhaps an "English Sinner".

As "It Happens", and at the very real risk of being "Immemorable", I'd much rather "Take The Car".

Yours, "Spreading The Net", with "Concern",

D Philpott

Dear Pilpot,

We do think *'That'* you haven't quite got it the *'Right Way Round'*, as you seem to think.

'If Only If' you had checked with us first. *'Sometimes'*, down *'Villier Street'*, *'It Happens'* that *'Everything'* is misunderstood. So, as *'Francis Said'*, it is *'Clearly'* obvious that *'Alice'* and *'Derek'* thought they could *'Take The Car'*, or as they call it, *'The Sedan'*, for a drive, but they were then involved in a *'Smash Up'*.

No motorbike was involved as *'Virginia'*, that *'Weekend'*, had gone *'Round The World'*. *'If Only If'* they had decided instead to go for an *'Ice Cream'* *'This Afternoon'*, they would not have had such a *'Bitter End'*.

Now we are having to go to *'Uncle Joe's Funeral'* *'This Afternoon'*, as they ran him over.

Overall, we are wondering if your letter is a bit of a *'Wind-Up'*. You seem to be living *'In A Vacuum'* but, as *'Molly Says'*, you do seem to have *'Nixon's Eyes'*, so we don't mind.

~~Chatgpt~~

Yours, etc,

McTells

Dear The ~~Rut Range~~ Groove Farm,

Your inability to "Stand Another Sunny Day" may have "clouded" the worst pop meteorological claim since Messrs Walker declared, "The Sun Aint Gonna Shine Anymore", The ~~Hollow Hacienda~~ Groove Farm.

Just because "your feet keep slipping off the ground" in the summertime, The ~~Grease Plantation~~ Groove Farm, doesn't mean that "It Always Rains On Sunday".

Obviously, I feel "Sad For You", The ~~Gouge Acreage~~ Groove Farm. "I Don't Blame You" for your dubious durable day of rest drizzle diatribe, and in the "Back Of My Mind" hope that you don't "feel menaced".

Yours "waiting for something to happen",

D. Philpott

Dear Mr. Philpott,

Thank you kindly for taking the time to write to us, and we hope this reply helps to clear a few things up for you.

Ensconced within Bristol's muesli-belt community of Totterdown, we were fully cognisant of all matters eco. Contrary to the commonly-held belief that "It Always Rains on Sunday" was from a film title, it was a prescient nod to climate change, as were "God's Tears", ergo "Heaven Is Blue". In fact, "My Feet Keep Slipping" was an attempt at a skit on the same theme, prompted by an accident involving persistent wet foliage on Andrew's doorstep.

Sadly, the environmental message fell on deaf ears, and it took the themes of summertime and surfing to finally build the group a following.

Yours, 'only very slightly menaced',

The Groove Farm.

Dear 14 ~~Crystallised Kaolas~~ Iced Bears,

Unless it's "The Wonder of Coincidence", I "Take It" from your "Holland" song that you are "Inside" Amsterdam, 14 ~~Powdery Polars~~ Iced Bears.

If so, 14 ~~Drizzled Grizzlies~~ Iced Bears, to "find the way to the window and sit a day or four" in the "Red Now" has me "Coming Down" to the conclusion that you are "Falling Backwards" into the "oldest profession".

I urge you, 14 ~~Preserved Pandas~~ Iced Bears - please don't diddle about on a crossroads. Cease these "Unhappy Days" or be "smiling and sore til the end".

"Come get me" if you need a lift "in the morning".

Yours, hoping it "makes you wonder",

D Philpott

Dear Mr Philpott,

Ha! You don't know how close this came to reality. I'm scared to know what other secrets of mine you're sensing!

I was actually living in Amsterdam in 2008 and had to move. The only place I could afford was above a brothel in the non-tourist Red Light district with naked ladies dancing in the window of the ground floor. I would have had to share the toilet (no door) outside my tiny room with all the staff and clients. Even Lou Reed wouldn't have moved in there!

Sorry to worry you earlier. I'm OK, with very little intention of going on the game.

If I do, the first one's free on me.

Yours,

Robert Sekula

Dear Prolapse,

Even if adept at galloping a "flat velocity curve", I am getting quite psychotic now concerning "Snappy Horse" and bookies' favourite, "Little Choosie Suzy".

The poor beast, forced to run not on grass but instead "cruisin' roon the bends, tearin' up the tarmac careerin' roon again", could suffer "Pointless Walks To Dismal Places" such as the blacksmiths to repair torn hooves and for a "Return Of Shoes".

Yours, fearing that you are "never comin' back",

D Philpott

Dear Mr. Philpott,

Congratulations; you are the first person to engage with our lyrics and decipher their true meaning.

All our songs were written in the bookies. Unfortunately, after many failed attempts at gambling responsibly, we had to do what every other gambler does - form a band and make money.

We managed to scramble enough money together from the first advance to put an each-way bet on a rank outsider.

As you can see from our various attempts at creating music through the years, our luck on the horses has not been good.

Expect a new album every year until I die (which being brought up on a Scottish diet could be sooner rather than later).

Yours sincerely,

Mr Michael Derrick of Prolapse.

Dear ~~Hyperbolic Metropolis Quartet~~ Mega City Four

Rather than a severe attack of the truth, what you've got is a "Disturbed" view of "January". The "pages thick in your calendar" must have been printed "On Another Planet" if its "Alternative Arrangements" indicate that "Christmas is years away"!

Please don't shoot the "Messenger" or hold a "Grudge" because I carried on when I should have stopped ~~Dynamic District Delta~~ Mega City Four.

I look forward to hearing back by letter or e-mail, although it's not the only way we can communicate.

Yours, "Miles Apart" and "Wasting My Breath",

D. Philpott

Dear Mr Philpott,

Thank you for your letter.

I don't know about you, but January for me these days is a grim, grey month spent sitting indoors doing my year-end accounts, sipping wine and watching Netflix. Not very rock 'n' roll, I know, but it helps me get into the extremely miserable post-Xmas state I crave.

I always think that if I start the year on the lowest ebb possible the rest of the year can only get better!

Talking of Xmas... it used to be fun in the 1970s, what with power cuts, Evel Knievel toys and what I consider to be 'real' fairy lights. None of this low voltage LED nonsense; I'm talking proper electric shocks when you change the bulbs.

I once tried fixing the wire with some choccy block while they were still plugged in and the shock threw me across the room!

You only do that once in your life.

Yuletide is all a bit too much like hard work these days since we rescued a fuzzy black German Spitz doggo that likes attacking everyone that comes into our house. Last year he bit my mum and even though my Aunty Margaret tried to talk to him sternly in his native language (she lived in Germany for about 30 years) he still persists in terrorising all but me and my missus.

So you see, the best "Christmas IS years away"...but it's about 50 years in the past.

Sod email & 'snail' mail, do you have a wurdle?

Kind regards,

Gerry

Dear ~~Puppet Potpourri~~ Dolly Mixture,

You must "Remember This", ~~Figurine Fusion~~ Dolly Mixture, and "Never Let It Go".

My "Understanding" is that even if "Jane's eyebrows may be the best thing in town", to shoot them up is unlikely to "make them frown" or be a "Dream Come True", ~~Marionette Mashup~~ Dolly Mixture. Instead, ~~Action Figure Amalgam~~ Dolly Mixture, expect what lies "Round The Corner" and down the line to be a patting down by a police officer ("he's so frisky") followed by "Night After Night" divided by a wall from a "Welcome Home" where the "Grass Is Greener"!

Yours, with all the information you want to know,

D. Philpott

Dear Mr. Packpan I mean Philpott,

Thank you for your letter enquiring about whether shooting up Jane's eyebrows would in fact make them frown.

Unfortunately we never did find out the answer to that question as it was only an intention and we actually never felt the urge to shoot up anyone else's eyebrows to make them frown again. Therefore there was never a need for a police officer to frisk any member of the band. I'm sorry I can't be of more help on this subject and I beg you not to try it at home.

Regards,

Rachel from Teddy Mishmash,

I mean Dolly Mixture!!

Dear The ~~Teen Trimmers~~ Boy Hairdressers,

Your slumber hallucinations are inaccurate; I don't run a dairy and all butterfat placed in my Nescafe is from Aldi.

Your statement therefore, The ~~School Age Stylists~~ Boy Hairdressers, "I dream of your cream", should by no means be amongst "all your finest memories".
Yours,

D Philpott

Dear Phil,

Thank you ~~very much~~ for your ~~legal~~ letter / ~~email / gift~~ .
I ~~liked / loved /~~ received / it ~~and will respond properly in due course~~ .

~~Do /~~ Don't keep in touch

~~Yours~~ sincerely,

Francis Macdonald

PS: You must remember Norman, Jim, Joe & Raymond were a lot older than me when I drummed with them. I didn't really know what was going on. ~~Sorry~~ I can't be more help.

Dear The Popinjays,

My friend, Leonard Rowe, a bashful carpenter, was commissioned to build a "Perfect Dream Home" for a client who wanted to go "Back To The Beginning", and, "Thinking About The Weather", live in Bournemouth.

"Please Let Me Go" on, The Popinjays. They wanted the lightest, most decorative "Bang Up To Date" timber, but Len was "overwhelmed and frankly scared as hell" by the B&Q chap and bought MDF without "Fine Lines".

"Slowly I Reach" the conclusion, The Popinjays, that there's nothing worse than a timid man that can't get wood. Ergo, "just a shy guy looking for a two-ply" is no excuse to be "Laughing At It All".

Yours, hoping you don't think "It Doesn't Matter".

D. Philpott

Dear Mr Philpott,

Clearly this does matter, to all concerned. Your friend, Mr Rowe, has already displayed some confusing behaviour in that he has interpreted a set of song titles to mean that he was to rush to B&Q and buy some MDF. If he had taken the time to listen a bit more carefully to the instructions, he would have heard that this was exactly the kind of behaviour that we were advising against. Like so many that have come before, he has misunderstood our seemingly cheerful delivery and jaunty tunes to lull himself into a false sense of security and an urge to comply with the consumer society. We can understand his predicament to some extent; the modern world can be a confusing place. As a band we have always followed a DIY ethic; whether that was writing our own songs, booking shows, making the posters or driving ourselves to gigs. It's DIY but, unfortunately for Mr Rowe, not in a B&Q way.

We hope that Mr Rowe has enough good sense and the ability to tap into his inner resources sufficiently to turn his life around and stop relying on cheap double entendres and hanging out at retail parks. We wish him well.

Wendy & Polly Popinjay

*Upon completion of this correspondence it was discovered that Mr Philpott had through no fault of his own used incorrect source material. It was however mutually agreed by both parties that they couldn't be bothered to start again.

Dear The Woodentops,

I am Well Well Well aware that "Everything Breaks" but I bought some Hush Puppies online and they fell apart just a few days into "Everyday Living"; in fact they didn't even "Take Me Through The Night".

I was advised that to return them would be inadvisable but decided to "Do It Anyway" which was a "Good Thing" - I was, "I'm Delighted" to report, sent a replacement pair last Tuesday or Wednesday.

They can say what they want but "It Will Come" as no surprise that you also found your sole in the crowd and sent it straight way back to Amazon.

Your Special Friend,

D Philpott

Dear Derek,

Thank you for your letter. Yes, I do write titles that are simple little lines like normal conversation and thanks for juggling them into a bit of fun. I never was very lyrically imaginative. I didn't do school really like you must have. Mainly band rehearsals and young offenders' prison which I did learn a lot in to be honest. Not to worry; I wasn't there very long. My appeal worked out and you know what? The really sweet chaps that arrested me said if they knew the result would be this they'd have let me go. It was DS Ring & Reeve that came straight to my holding cell with the forms to begin the appeal. See? Not all police are bad. In fact apart from one I've never met a nasty one; always helpful. One, now retired, PC Barry Critchley, used to come to mine for coffee and tell me John Peel and Ian Dury stories and stuff like how he recorded the sound of the ghost opera singer in the old night club on Clapham High Street and did I know there was a recording studio, everything in there ready to go but bricked in by a wall? So it's still there. Funny we called ourselves The Woodentops with all this police talk. Alice's idea - she actually was literate. Very. A Woodentop is a slang for a cop. Woodentops can equal cops, hence Lee Scratch Perry's idea for our second album title: 'Woodenfoot Cops on the Highway'. A clever play on words, using Lee Scratch as cut up machine, which he was - R.I.P that genius - instead of the David Bowie Burroughs Gysin cut up technique with paper typewriter and scissors. However it was not our reason for choosing the band name, the police. We were looking for an anti-name like 'West Wickhams'; an anti name of today's anti names. Still, to see a race horse galloping away there called Woodentops when it did was fun. We chose the name because the Woodentops puppet show defined our generation. 60s. That was the crap they gave us kids. Now they get adventure time. Actually even that is now retro but brilliant anyway. It's not Watch With Mother, more like wave a fan at mother because she's fainted, My eyes, this phone, did I say farted?

But yes those song titles of the 80s. As you can see I've not improved. The Woodentops' first review in the New Musical Express; can you imagine how excited we were? A little tiny show, bottom of the bill at Dingwalls old club, excited squeals from the just 20 year old musicians. Ambition realised!

"Rolo is a musical and lyrical flannel". Oh. Then a big picture of me hand clapping as we did in a Flamenco clapping and anarchic folk chaos with another great simple title "Everybody" - why I was clapping. "Rolo clapping himself" blah blah. Guess we were too young to know that writers are looking for word cannon fodder to make their way up the ladder of fun insult hurling. Why not? Good fun.

But then here we are decades later still kicking everybody's asses with invention. The thing is, that's where the difficulty lies. Write stuff like everybody else is and yep you sell more beers at the bar. The Liquor God likes you. These days the promoter will say, "nice to see you again after all these years, so I expect you'll be playing all the old hits?!!" "Yessir we'll be playing the old hits". Actually as few as possible, even if you still enjoy to play them because they've never been anything but shit hot. But some are older than any dog could live Derek. I suppose they mean things to people like "When I was young free single and could get shit faced with my friends get laid a lot and nowadays it's all bollocks". Tricky, never went to music or art school but trying to come up with stuff, even if I need to take 15 years off to make new life to write about because I don't make it up, is hard as ever. Don't worry, I went electronic and made 99% instrumentals with much better titles than for Woodentops. But heres a funny thing: apart from having the unofficial hit that invented just about every baggy trouser E munching kid in the UK with Why Why Why, (another corny easy off the gob title), I was now free entry in every nightclub door you can think of. Lifetime free entry card to Ministry of Sound etc.. My quest for anonymity blown because my little bit of dancing fun was often blown by being recognised and a crowd of people going heeeey! now dancing with me and around me like suddenly I was on TV. Better notch up my dance moves! People would say 'your club floor music is like Woodentops mate! I hear it!'. Failure!! I am trying to move on here darling. Like my hero Miles Davis or Prince who would only stay in one creative place for a split second. Geminis like me. Don't care if it's a success or not or if the Liquor God is happy. It's about art and creativity and reacting to the times, not one moment back when, Derek. Anyway my new single 'Ride a Cow Like A Horse' is doing very well. A fun stripped to the swimming trunks remix or 'unmix', of which is playing right now in Pike's hotel swimming poolside as we speak, in Ibiza. The most ultra hip poolside in the world. Perhaps it is like lift music for that scenario but we designed it for that at mix. Because not many people are lounging about in space. Which is what the song is really about. The chap Mike Massimo whose life ambition was to go to space and work on the Hubble Space Telescope and was sent to update it because the telescope thanks to a highly successful public appeal survived decommissioning. Mike's dream came true but when he got there he broke it. Oops!! Nasa told him to smash it more to break in to the electronics to complete the update. "You can achieve your dreams but the outcome may not be as you had hoped", the message there. Music with no business plan to sell liquor is hot juice and to be the winner of a Jukebox Jury by Youth and Steve Lillywhite is gold. In 2023 I mean, that kind of thing makes it all worth while. I think my titles have improved on the new upcoming LP but I just know you could have fun with the titles though, like 'Dream on", "Ride a Cloud", "The Fishermen Leave At Dusk", "Traversing Heartbreak", "Too Good to Stay", "Lately", "Don't Stop", "Can't Stand Still", "Hotel", "Saturday" and the appropriate for this rant "Liquid Thinking". There's more but you can see I predicted you coming with your titles game Derek. I think it's really good fun and I hope you enjoyed my reply. Meanwhile the comment in the example you sent from Tulalah Gosh asking about is the lady in the test card bored? Cracked me up.

I'm not joking when I say it's a pleasure to be asked to contribute an answer and I hope you like it. I thought shall I just free form on you yes, just Do It Anyway!

Love ®¬.

P.S. Don't worry I type like the wind.

Dear The Servants,

I was sorry to hear you'd spilt your Chinese dinner, perhaps during a night of "Self Destruction" commencing at The Adam & Eve on Uxbridge Road.

I too have had "squid on my stomach exploding fat" after ordering "The Complete Works", and have drank from the ~~grail~~ ale enough to pour cream in the ashtray lying on my belly pretending I was a whale.

They should make a ~~statue~~ statute against those in a Hayes where "Bad Habits Die Hard", for the "Thin Skinned". Or "we could stay at home and never leave"...

Yours, hoping to have been "Transparent",

D Philpott

Dear Mr Philpott,

How kind of you to write to me. I was beginning to think nobody cared. That said, I've been beginning to think that way since C86 came out.

I am humbled by your discursive familiarity with my back catalogue. And it is always heartwarming to find mention of my old home town - Hayes, Middlesex. I regret, though, that your obvious talent for wilfully obscure allusiveness is bound to be lost on many. As the line from Hamlet goes, you provide caviar to the general.

Please find enclosed a copy of my latest album, 'My Beautiful England'. I hope you like it. If you are the type of person to whom it matters, I hope you will find the tenor of the sentiments expressed at least broadly compatible with your own. If you find yourself only trendily aggrieved, of course, up yours.

Sincerely,

David Westlake (The Servants)

Dear ~~Segmentshack~~ Chapterhouse,

I took my first trip abroad in sixteen years this April, ~~Bookpartbuilding~~ Chapterhouse, as the rain was "Falling Down" in Blighty.

Torremolinos seemed ideal after a summer chill, but I *was* losing touch with my mind on the way to fly and could not "Keep The Faith" after an hour at Easyjet's check-in desk. Your observations "You Find It Out When You Lose Your Life", and "When The World Lets You Down" seemed particularly prescient.

Indeed, it *did* mutate into a confusion trip when despite asking to speak to a greater power, with my hand luggage in my arms, I suffered "Time Speeds" owing to priority boarding passengers.

Yours, now sat in safe at home,

D. Philpott

Dear Dr Pott,

It is difficult for me to adequately express how joyful I was on receiving your remarkable letter. I can say without hesitation that you are the first and only person I have encountered to truly understand the gravity of what I was attempting to convey when writing "On The Way To Fly". I can only assume that you must be a Dr. of Literature, such is your level of insight and emotional maturity. It is not every day that I am introduced to someone with your enviable gift of a vision that can gaze directly into a person's soul.

Phil... I would go as far as to say that you are a seer, a sage, a necromancer, even. Reading your words was like staring at myself in the mirror and that is an experience for which I will be eternally thankful. I hope I'm not being overfamiliar by addressing you by your first name but I feel as though we have a strong kinship. It is incredibly heart warming to know that there is a person out there in this world that truly "gets" where I'm coming from.

Yours in gratitude and brotherhood,

Stephen Patman

Dear The ~~Pelletpistols~~ Popguns,

I used to visit my friend Max Shayler but "We Don't Go Round There Anymore" – he wanted to "Get Out" of safety measures and do Guy Fawkes displays "Under Starlight". He nearly "Beat Me Up" for threatening to report him for "Carrying The Fire"works.

I'm not "So Cold" though, The ~~AirUzis~~ Popguns. When "someone makes an offer" I tend not to "Leave It Alone".

However, in order that you may "Stay Alive", I must fully disclose that I am not a trained X-Ray radiologist, so must decline your invitation to "Come inside, take a look around me".

Yours, hoping that you appreciate the "Gesture",

D Philpott

The Popguns
Popgun Mansions
4 Poplar Avenue
Popton-on-Sea

27 August 2023

Dear Mr. Philpott,

Thank you for getting in touch.

Unfortunately, time is not on our side. In fact, for a properly considered reply, you would undoubtedly be Waiting for the Winter.

Yours Apologetically,

Pat Popgun

Send that idiot this to get rid of him but tear this bit off before you send it or you'll never hear the end of it

Dear Catherine Wheel
D & D PHILPOTT

The
End

New Edition!

Dear Mr Pop Star

D&D PHILPOTT

Bonkers letters to pop stars

with hilarious replies

from the actual artists!

Do shopping

Write to follow

pop stars:

1) The blonde

plays guitar in t

new roman

Dear Mr. Kershaw

A PENSIONER WRITES

DEREK PHILPOTT *(with help from his neighbour Wilf Turnbull)*

Letters to pop stars from

a retired member of the public...

with GENUINE REPLIES

from the artists themselves!

Includes 16 glorious pages of full-colour Philpottery!

Grammar Free
in the U.K.

D & D PHILPOTT

Bonkers letters to
& from U.K. punks
during Lockdown

MUSICIANS
AGAINST
HOMELESSNESS

Tell Sham 69 they can't go down the pub
Write to Max Splodge about beer/crisps
Car in rut. Email The Ruts for help
Message Corba